DOUBT AND DOGMA
IN MARIA EDGEWORTH
by *Mark D. Hawthorne*

UNIVERSITY OF FLORIDA PRESS / GAINESVILLE, 1967

EDITORIAL COMMITTEE

Humanities Monographs

T. WALTER HERBERT, *Chairman*
Professor of English

G. PAUL MOORE
Professor of Speech

CHARLES W. MORRIS
Professor of Philosophy

REID POOLE
Professor of Music

C. A. ROBERTSON
Professor Emeritus of English

MELVIN E. VALK
Professor of German

AUBREY L. WILLIAMS
Professor of English

AUTHOR'S NOTE

There is no standard edition of Maria Edgeworth's fiction. Since she revised many of her novels after their first publication, I have used the first edition unless there is no significant variation of the text. In those cases in which the final edition is identical with the first, I have used the Routledge Edition of *The Tales and Novels by Maria Edgeworth* (London, 1893). In the following list of abbreviations, I have indicated only the volume in which the work in question may be found. Unless otherwise noted, each work is by Maria Edgeworth and was published in London. See the Bibliography for those works which have been useful in my analysis of Miss Edgeworth's fiction but which are not referred to in the text by means of abbreviations.

Belinda—Belinda (2nd ed.; 3 vols.; 1802).
Essays—Richard Lovell Edgeworth, *Essays on Professional Education* (2nd ed.; 1812).
Fashionable Life—Tales of Fashionable Life, First Series (3rd ed.; 3 vols.; 1809).
Griselda—The Modern Griselda (1st ed.; 1805).
Hare—Augustus J. C. Hare (ed.), *The Life and Letters of Maria Edgeworth* (2 vols.; Boston, 1895).
Inglis-Jones—Elisabeth Inglis-Jones, *The Great Maria: A Portrait of Maria Edgeworth* (1959).
Leonora—Leonora (1st ed.; 2 vols.; 1806).
Letters—Letters for Literary Ladies (Routledge Edition, Vol. VIII).
Memoirs—Memoirs of Richard Lovell Edgeworth, Esq., Begun by Himself and Concluded by His Daughter (1st ed.; 2 vols.; 1820).
Moral Tales—Moral Tales for Young People (Routledge Edition, Vol. I).
Newby—P. H. Newby, *Maria Edgeworth* (Denver, 1950).
Oliver—Grace A. Oliver, *A Study of Maria Edgeworth with Notes of Her Father and Friends* (2nd ed.; 1882).
Ormond—Harrington, A Tale; and Ormond, A Tale (1st ed.; 2 vols.; 1817).
Patronage—Patronage (1st ed.; 4 vols.; 1814).
Popular Tales—Popular Tales (Routledge Edition, Vol. II).
Practical Education—Maria Edgeworth and Richard Lovell Edgeworth, *Practical Education* (1st ed.; 2 vols.; 1798).
Slade—Bertha Coolidge Slade, *Maria Edgeworth, 1767-1849: A Bibliographical Tribute* (1937).
"Vivian"—"Vivian" (Routledge Edition, Vol. V).

CONTENTS

INTRODUCTION

While many studies of the history of the British novel respectfully devote a few pages to Maria Edgeworth (1767-1849), the tendency has been to accept clichés about her influence on Scott and her dependence upon her father, then nonchalantly to assign her to oblivion. In comparison with Jane Austen's, her fiction has inevitably suffered, but of her fifteen books published between 1800 and 1817, only one did not have a second edition within a year of its original publication. Such popularity brought widespread recognition. She associated with the finest minds, both of England and France; she was lionized by the fashionable circles of London, Edinburgh, and Paris; and she enjoyed a reading audience that spanned three continents. In spite of this popularity in her own day, her name is now seldom mentioned, and her books do little more than collect dust.

This neglect has grown from misreading and has led to a misrepresentation of her place in literary history. In short, she deserved the popularity that her contemporaries bestowed upon her both as an artist and as an original thinker.

Maria Edgeworth has two distinct reputations. She was a pioneer in the field of education. She shared her interest in education with her father, a man who realized the imperfections of Rousseau's theories and tried to reduce education to an experimental science. Before the collaboration of this remarkable amateur scientist and his talented daughter, only two significant educational treatises based on empiricism had appeared in England. Locke's *Some Thoughts Concerning Education* (1693), as Dr. Johnson remarked, "has been tried often enough, but is very imperfect";[1] Rousseau's *Émile* (1762) electrified many Englishmen but proved too insubstantial to be practical. Mr. Edgeworth, in fact, attempted to educate his oldest son as a second Émile, but the result was disastrous. Afterwards he turned to experimentation. Any technique that led to the desired ends was isolated and codified until he was able to supervise Miss Edgeworth's composition of *Practical Education* (1798), "la victoire de l'esprit philosophique et de la méthode

---

1. Boswell, *Life of Samuel Johnson*, p. 849. Complete information on textual references is found in the Bibliography.

1

expérimentale baconienne."[2] When this treatise appeared, the English and French were given the most important work on general education that appeared in eighteenth-century England. What had been practical in Locke's and Rousseau's theories was transformed into a step-by-step procedure that any parent could follow. Now partly outdated, *Practical Education* was greatly influential during the first half of the nineteenth century and exerted such an influence on later educational theorists that many of its principles have become the stock in trade of modern educators.

Maria Edgeworth, the educational pioneer, was also a novelist. Primarily concerned with the didactic novel, she tried to combine her interest in education and her interest in fiction. Ironically, the two novels that are still widely read—*Castle Rackrent* and *The Absentee*—are exceptions to her usual writing practice. Much of our misunderstanding of her career is the result of judging her in the light of these exceptions and damning the bulk of her work as inferior. This is like praising *Troilus and Criseyde* by ignoring *The Canterbury Tales*.

A study of the educational treatises written under the direct supervision of her father, a comparison of the assumptions of these works with her own opinions that emerge from her fiction, and an examination of the movement of her thought away from her father's—this three-fold method will give us a way to measure her development and a norm by which to analyze the structure of the novels and short stories. Sensitive to the novel's structural and symbolic possibilities, Miss Edgeworth frequently wrote on two distinct levels. Superficially, she was didactic, purely and simply. It is this level that repels many twentieth-century scholars, for she could be as crudely dogmatic as the authors of *Caleb Williams* and *Self-Control*. Second, she was skillful and subtle, probing the depths of psychology and philosophy with unusual candor. *Belinda*, for example, may be damned as overly didactic and poorly written, or it may be praised for its remarkable restraint and intellectual subtlety. On the first level, she used the novel as a teaching device, the surface embracing her father's dogma. On the second, she advanced her own doubts through structure and symbolism. Sustaining this continuous dialogue, she created from the didactic novel a form of fiction that is at once outspoken and subdued, a form in which meaning arises from the tension between didactic surface

2. Roddier, J.-J. *Rousseau en Angleterre au XVIIIᵉ siècle*, p. 172.

and symbolic structure. Through this tension, often ironic in nature, she pleased both her father, a representative late eighteenth-century rationalist, and herself, an early nineteenth-century romantic. Whenever one of her novels or short stories appears to lack surface cohesion, we should suspect that she was developing a coherent substructure of opinions that differ, often very radically, from the principles she appears to have been teaching. She wrote long before the age of James, Woolf, and Joyce—she had not learned to make a tightly woven texture that combines surface and image, explicit statement and implicit meaning.

The most widely circulated misunderstanding of Maria Edgeworth's work concerns her supposed dependence upon her father. This dependence is said to have resulted in a lack of intellectual and imaginative freedom and in a sweeping condemnation of imagination and passion.[3] Perhaps she inadvertently invited this view from her description of Mr. Edgeworth's editing her fiction: "Whenever I thought of writing any thing, I always told him my first rough plans; and always, with the instinct of a good critic, he used to fix immediately upon that, which would best answer the purpose—'Sketch that, and shew it to me'—These words, from the experience of his sagacity, never failed to inspire me with hope of success. It was then sketched. Sometimes, when I was fond of a particular part, I used to dilate on it in the sketch; but to this he always objected—'I don't want any of your painting—none of your drapery!—I can imagine all that—let me see the bare skeleton.'"

Later she continued: "His skill in *cutting*—his decision in criticism was peculiarly useful to me. His ready invention and infinite resources, when I had run myself into difficulties or absurdities, never failed to extricate me at my utmost need. It was the happy experience of this, and my consequent reliance on his ability, decision, and perfect truth, that relieved me from the vacillation and anxiety to which I was so much subject. . . . He inspired in my mind a degree of hope and confidence, essential in the first instance to the full exertion of the mental powers, and necessary to ensure perseverance in any occupation" (*Memoirs*, II, 344-47). But an analysis of her thematic structures, the interplay of characters, and the use of symbolism will demonstrate that she did not

3. See, for example, Grey, "Society According to Maria Edgeworth," p. 298; Armytage, "Little Women," p. 249; Baker, *History of the English Novel*, pp. 21-22; Allen, *English Novel*, pp. 98-102; or Stevenson, *English Novel*, p. 184.

accept her father's basic premises until she incorporated the demands of the passions into his educational theory.

In this analysis of Miss Edgeworth's intellectual and artistic development, I have omitted extended discussions of *Castle Rackrent* and *The Absentee*, neither of which is as illustrative of her development as are less widely known works. I have followed the dates of the first editions for the overall arrangement of this study. There are, however, some difficulties. In *Popular Tales* (1804) and in the First Series of *Tales of Fashionable Life* (1809) each story was followed by the date of composition. I have used these dates within my analysis of the particular volumes in order to put the stories in a logical sequence, even though a few of these dates indicate that the stories may predate earlier volumes. This question of dates of composition in relation to the development of Miss Edgeworth's thought is treated in detail in Chapter Four. Finally, I have discussed Miss Edgeworth's career only from 1795 to 1817, thus omitting the very fine novel *Helen*, published in 1834. Since the intellectual and artistic structure of this final novel shows no remarkable advance over *Ormond*, the novel in which she finally reconciled her father's assumptions and her own beliefs, a discussion of it would be anticlimactic.

CHAPTER ONE

I n her earliest publications, *Letters for Literary Ladies* (1795) and *Practical Education* (1798), Maria Edgeworth wrote on education. These books give us the assumptions against which she reacted in her fiction, but to put an analysis of them on a firm basis, we must briefly look into her childhood. If the habits instilled in her as a child are in agreement with the educational theory of her earliest books, the argument that she and her father closely collaborated is justified, but if there is reason to think—as indeed there is—that her childhood was other than the theory would lead us to believe, we have our first ground for questioning this conventional view. Furthermore, if we can establish the assumptions of these earliest books and then trace the author's evolution from them only to find her later suddenly repeating them, we have our second ground for questioning the conventional view.

The family mansion at Edgeworthstown was Maria Edgeworth's home from her fifteenth birthday to the day of her death. Isolated from the "fashionable world," this Irish hamlet was completely dominated by one strong personality—Richard Lovell Edgeworth. Inventor, civil engineer, amateur scientist, philanthropist, friend of poets and statesmen, conversationalist—Mr. Edgeworth was many things, but most of all he was a father and an educator, a man who successfully combined love for his children and devotion to experimental science. The offspring of his four prolific marriages, Mr. Edgeworth's children transformed the sedate old mansion into a nursery where all that was needed for experiments with educational methods was available. Using his first twelve children as guinea pigs, he tried to reduce education to an experimental science. As a father, he wanted to provide the best education for his large family, so he turned the nursery into a laboratory. His younger children were the subjects of experiments designed to determine the applicability of earlier theories and his older children were analysts who collected the seemingly endless data from the experiments.

In his memoirs, Mr. Edgeworth explained that this interest in education partly originated from an unforgettable childhood experience. He was so mischievous a youngster that only his crippled mother could control him. Because she was unable to whip him and because scolding was useless, she treated him like a rational being; she reasoned with him, pointing out the undesirable ends of imprudent acts and showing him the reasons for her concern. Once when he almost killed his elder brother in a fit of anger, she calmly said: "You . . . have naturally a violent temper: if you grow up to be a man without learning to govern it, it will be impossible for you then to command yourself; and there is no knowing what crime you may in a fit of passion commit, and how miserable you may in consequence of it become. . . . Instead of speaking to you as I do at this moment, I might punish you severely; but I think it better to teach you to command your temper; nobody can do that for you, so well as you can do it for yourself" (*Memoirs*, I, 27-29).

But in spite of the determination that this experience gave him, Mr. Edgeworth failed to curb his "passionate temper." Years later, he was so inflamed by Rousseau's *Émile* that he attempted to educate his eldest son according to the Frenchman's plan of not curbing nature. With *Émile* as his Bible and the eccentric Thomas Day as his mentor, he turned his back on the objections of his friends and family and reared young Richard as a noble savage. The result was inevitable. "He was bold, free, fearless, generous; he had a ready and keen use of all his senses, and of his judgment. But he was not disposed to *obey*: his exertions generally arose from his own will; and, though he was what is commonly called good-tempered and good-natured, though he generally pleased by his looks, demeanour, and conversation, he had too little deference for others, and he shewed an invincible dislike to control" (*Memoirs*, I, 179). As young Richard became more and more uncontrollable, Mr. Edgeworth was forced to admit that he had let his reason be lulled by Rousseau's "charms of eloquence." Eventually defying even his father, the boy kicked the dust of England from his shoes and settled in America, a land more friendly to noble savages.

Mr. Edgeworth then assumed the role of a rationalist. The determination to live up to this new role well illustrates what psychologists call "over-compensation." Young Richard proved to him the imperfections of Rousseau's system, and he strove to educate his seventeen other children to be useful members of a civilized society. He then remembered the calm words of his mother, and henceforth his children were treated like rational beings who must eliminate all passion and emotion in order to live virtuously and prudently.

Although he loved his children, Mr. Edgeworth regarded them with the detached benevolence of a clinical psychologist and sought to mold useful, rational, and prudent citizens. Disregarding Locke's warning that "God has stamped certain characters upon men's minds, which, like their shapes, may perhaps be a little mended; but can hardly be totally altered and transformed into the contrary,"[1] he ignored his children's temperaments and taught by precept and example that reason is the sole guide to human conduct. He calculated the behavioral effects of certain stimuli, then experimented. Recording the experiments, he collected material that, he believed, was useful because it was the result of successful experiments. That is, he began with self-evident laws, reduced them by Baconian induction, then judged the results by utilitarian values. In short, he attempted the impossible. Yet many years later Miss Edgeworth still praised him: "If I were obliged to rest on any single point, my father's credit as a lover of truth, and his utility as a philanthropist and a philosophical writer, it should be on his having made this first record of experiments in education" (*Memoirs*, II, 186).

But this rationalism did not seem to affect Miss Edgeworth until she had already formed deeply engrained habits. Born on January 1, 1767, she lived with her mother until 1773. During this time her father was seldom at home; he was too interested in his son's education to let ordinary domestic affairs distract him. Besides, Mrs. Edgeworth's nagging had alienated her husband's affections to the point that he had fallen in love with the beautiful Honora Sneyd. So long as the first Mrs. Edgeworth lived, rationalism could not have been an influence on Maria. Her father was in the midst of rearing a second Émile, and she lived with a passionate and temperamental woman who continually lamented that she had rushed into an imprudent marriage. In fact, it was not until after the first Mrs. Edgeworth's death and Mr. Edgeworth's hasty marriage to Miss Sneyd in June, 1773, that the first traces of rationalism could have entered her education.

But in 1775 Miss Edgeworth attended a boarding-school kept by a Mrs. Latiffiere in Derby where she remained until 1780 when

1. *Some Thoughts Concerning Education*, p. 43.

she was sent to Mrs. Davis' boarding school in London. In neither school was any effort made to control her already vivid imagination or to develop her still nascent powers of reasoning. On the contrary, at Mrs. Latiffiere's, Maria prepared her lessons in advance so that during playtime she could be "so absorbed in her book that she was 'perfectly deaf' to all around," and at night she entertained (and frightened) her companions with stories about such wildly imaginative characters as "an adventurer who had a mask made of the dried skin of a dead man's face" (*Oliver*, pp. 61-67). Not until 1782 did she permanently join her father and his third wife, Elizabeth Sneyd (Honora's sister), when they moved to Ireland. Only then was Miss Edgeworth influenced daily and directly by her father's strict rationalism.

Not having received even the scantiest rational education, Miss Edgeworth could hardly be expected to fit into her father's notion of the rational being. If anything, her early environment promoted regressions into fanciful and unbridled illusion and romance. She was small and not at all pretty, and her vivid imagination became a valued compensation for an otherwise drab life. But Mr. Edgeworth did not let this "dangerous" propensity pass unnoticed. In Ireland, he sought ascendancy over her mind. Attempting to give her rational habits, he made her "during many years . . . assist him in copying his letters of business, and in receiving his rents." In addition, when she was eighteen, he entrusted a younger brother to her care in order "to teach [her] the art of Education" (*Memoirs*, II, 15-25). By this time, the atmosphere at Edgeworthstown was rational and, under the influence of the third Mrs. Edgeworth, utilitarian, but Maria was stubborn. Mr. Edgeworth, for example, categorically condemned imagination, emotion, and passion; like Godwin, he accepted only reason and judgment as valid guides to happiness. When Maria analyzed this conclusion, she found that she was an impossible personality—imaginative and passionate yet prudent. "Her precepts were not the maxims of cold-hearted prudence," the fourth Mrs. Edgeworth wrote of her after her death, "but the result of her own experience in strong and romantic feeling" (Hare, I, 116). When she was in her fifties, she promised on her father's death bed to act prudently, but she was still the passionate girl who frightened her little companions with ghost stories.

Obviously, then, Miss Edgeworth was not the paragon of rationality idealized by her father, and the conventional view of complete collaboration between father and daughter is based on weak assumptions. There are serious differences between father and daughter, and we will see that these differences are essential to her craft of fiction, for once we can establish her father's assumptions by analyzing her earliest books, we can trace the slow evolution of her restless mind as she moved further and further from his assumptions. Later, when she was again made to codify his opinions, the contrast between the publications that immediately precede and follow and the publications in which she repeated Mr. Edgeworth's thoughts will be striking.

Miss Edgeworth's earliest publication, *Letters for Literary Ladies* (1795), is a defense of female education. The "Letter from a Gentleman to His Friend, Upon the Birth of a Daughter" presents the contemporary arguments against female education that the "Friend" debates in "Answer to the Preceding Letter." Avoiding Hannah More's and Mary Wollstonecraft's extreme views, the "Friend" defends female education on the bases that woman is as much a rational being as man and that without reason she cannot be fully happy. The final section of the slender volume is the "Letters of Julia and Caroline," a short epistolary story in which prudence is rewarded and imprudence punished. Already the consequences of her father's rationalism bothered Miss Edgeworth, who in this final section actually shows the pitfalls in the "Friend's" position.

Letters for Literary Ladies, like many of Miss Edgeworth's works, is deceptively straightforward. The second letter presents the assumptions that made Edgeworthstown unique, and the short fiction appears to illustrate them. From the inconsistency between the two parts we may conclude one of two things: either the book was carelessly written, or the inconsistency is functional. The first alternative is untenable: that the Edgeworths never published a "carelessly written" book can be documented from any phase of their careers. But the more probable second alternative necessitates finding the reason for the inconsistency. In the brief biographical sketch we saw that there was an essential difference between father and daughter. This difference is the same as the inconsistency between the parts of *Letters for Literary Ladies*: the father and the second letter accepted a system of rationalism that rejected the emotions, but the daughter and the short fiction gave the

9

emotions a place in human behavior. From this similarity we can argue that the opinions of the second letter are more likely Mr. Edgeworth's while those of the fiction are Miss Edgeworth's.

In the first letter, the "Gentleman" immediately states the anti-feminist belief that women are not entitled to a literary education. According to his illogical assumption, "it is not possible that women should ever be our equals in knowledge, unless you assert that they are far our superiors in natural capacity" (Letters, p. 428). Rather women should, as Rousseau so strongly advocated, remain in their proper sphere, the home. Because the "Gentleman" accepts social prejudice as philosophically sound, the belief that women are by nature inferior is, to him, undeniably true. He says, for example, that gentlemen cannot debate with a woman as an equal because men "see things as they are: but women must always see things through a veil, or cease to be women." Moreover, the "Gentleman" discounts those ladies who have been educated simply on the ground that they "dazzle and confound their critics" by entering upon subjects customarily reserved for men.

The "Gentleman" also disagrees with the rational doctrines that "morality should . . . be founded upon demonstration, not upon sentiment; and [that] we should not require human beings to submit to any laws or custom, without convincing their understandings of the universal utility of these political conventions." Interestingly, this position is similar to the one later developed in Miss Edgeworth's own compromise of reason and imagination. The "Gentleman," for example, touches on the very weakness of reason that she later analyzed in The Modern Griselda and Patronage: "The dignity of human nature, and the boasted free-will of rational agents, are high-sounding words, likely to impose upon the vanity of the fair sex, as well as upon the pride of ours; but if we analyze the ideas annexed to these terms, to what shall we reduce them? Reason in its highest perfection seems just to arrive at the certainty of instinct; and truth impressed upon the mind of early youth by the united voice of affection and authority, gives all the real advantages of the most investigating spirit of philosophy" (Letters, p. 432). But to say that she had already reached this stage in her intellectual development would be to exaggerate. She would hardly put her own opinions in the mouth of a character created only to knock down; she was much cleverer than that.

On the whole, the "Gentleman's" objections to the "enlightened" woman indirectly describe Miss Edgeworth's treatment of the ardent supporter of woman's rights, a frequent character in her early fiction. The "Gentleman" says that educated women are vain, shocking, undesirable as associates or wives, and indolent; Miss Edgeworth portrayed the "enlightened" woman in her fiction as socially unacceptable, whether she be a callous trickster like Mrs. Freke or a sentimental home-breaker like Lady Olivia. The "Gentleman," however, condemns all female education; Miss Edgeworth decried only the abuses. To the "Gentleman" any *literary* lady is a Circe; to Miss Edgeworth the true literary *lady* could be a Penelope. The one sees the educated woman as all bad; the other, as bad only if she flaunted the social code. They agree that excess is the greatest evil, but the "Gentleman" cannot conceive of moderation.

Miss Edgeworth obviously did not accept the "Gentleman's" position, but neither did she accept the arguments of the "Friend." Instead, she so carefully created the arguments of both the "Gentleman" and the "Friend" that each presents a valid case within the limits of his approach. The common sense of the "Gentleman" uncovers undeniable examples of abuses but offers no solutions; the "Friend's" rationalism is weakened by its theoretical nature. Miss Edgeworth saw through both sides.

The "Friend" expresses Mr. Edgeworth's belief that "till women learn to reason, it is vain that they acquire learning" (*Letters*, p. 440). A skillful debater, he carefully defines his terms to avoid the anti-feminist's greatest objections: ". . . when I use the term literary ladies, I mean women who have cultivated their understanding not for the purposes of parade, but with the desire to make themselves useful and agreeable. I estimate the value of a woman's abilities and acquirements, by the degree in which they contribute to her happiness" (*Letters*, p. 441). The "Friend" and the "Gentleman" thus hold at least one standard in common: the utility of female education is to determine its value. But this is the only concession that the "Friend" makes either to the "Gentleman" or to utilitarianism.

The "Gentleman's" principal objection to female education was his observation of the "enlightened" woman's reluctance to follow established moral and social codes; the "Friend" shows how the proper education will enable her to fulfill her moral and social responsibilities with the greatest happiness. Virtue and prudence will be taught by reason, and the prudent and learned ladies will slowly bring respect to female education. "It is scarcely to be supposed," he argues, "that a girl of good understanding would deliberately imitate the faults and follies which she hears ridiculed during her childhood, by those whom she esteems" (*Letters*, p. 443). Society does not, as the "Gentleman" contended, need to be altered if the educated woman learns prudence as well as literature and science. In fact, "women who have been well educated, far from despising domestic duties, will hold them in high respect; because they will see that the whole happiness of life is made up of the happiness of each particular day and hour, and that much of the enjoyment of these depends upon the punctual practice of these virtues which are more valuable than splendid" (*Letters*, p. 446). In this society, the wives might even reform their husbands.

The "Friend," describing the way he plans to educate his daughter (and incidently describing the way Mr. Edgeworth was then educating his younger children), foreshadows the system of *Practical Education*: "Believing, as I do, that woman, as well as man, may be called a bundle of habits, I shall be peculiarly careful, during my child's early education, to give her as many good habits as possible; by degrees as her understanding, that is to say as her knowledge and power of reasoning shall increase, I can explain the advantage of these habits, and confirm their power by the voice of reason." Children educated by habits and prejudices alone "will probably suspect that they have been deceived in all that they have been taught, and they will burst their bonds with indignation" (*Letters*, p. 447). The proper education will give the child "moral instinct" or "certain habits early acquired from education," but this instinct is weak and incomplete unless strengthened by reason. As in the systems of Locke and Rousseau, there is no virtue where there is no judgment; an impulsive act is neither moral nor immoral. In short, Mr. Edgeworth's moral philosophy was based on the intellectual fallacy.

Apparently, Mr. Edgeworth had not yet tempered his rationalism with the hedonistic association of the sensationists. Pleasure and pain form the keystone in Locke's ethical system: "Pleasure and pain and that which causes them,—good and evil, are the hinges on which our passions turn."[2] From Locke's crude hedonism, the pleasure-pain principle became a basic part of British

2. *Essay Concerning Human Understanding*, I.xx.3.

empiricism. Hume, for example, lucidly summarizes the viewpoint of this school in his *Treatise of Human Nature*: "The most probable hypothesis, which has been advanc'd to explain the distinction betwixt vice and virtue, and the origin of moral rights and obligations, is, that from a primary constitution of nature certain characters and passions, by the very view and contemplation, produce a pain, and others in like manner a pleasure."[3] Popularized further by Hartley, Abraham Tucker, Paley, and finally Bentham, this trend of Lockean thought threatened the strict rationalism of men like Richard Price, Godwin, and Mr. Edgeworth, who claimed that "the senses and the passions are strictly subordinate to the intellect."[4] It was this thread of empiricism, more than anything else, that developed into the romantic stress on feeling,[5] and Mr. Edgeworth abhorred anything that smacked of Rousseau as long as the memory of young Richard was still fresh in his mind.

If we trust Miss Edgeworth's account, Mr. Edgeworth believed (along with the French Rationalists, who so greatly influenced him at this time) that reason completely eclipses emotion and that ethics is a purely rational science. The logic behind Mr. Edgeworth's position is quite simple: emotion is by nature evil because it leads to imprudent acts; hence utilitarian ethics, which depends in part upon the emotions, is dangerous. What Mr. Edgeworth needed was rationalistic utilitarian ethics, a system in which merit was purely intellectual. But to confess that a man might choose virtue because it was pleasurable was to him tantamount to admitting that reason was not the sole guide to happiness. To admit that a woman can be passionate as well as prudent would support the "Gentleman's" arguments against female education. The plan of *Émile* ultimately results—as the "Friend" puts it—in a "delirium of passion." But in a rational education, "the experience of the past" forms a foundation that eliminates the faults caused by Rousseau's "fatal idea, that cunning and address are the natural resources of her sex"; the testimony of her father and brothers teaches a "realistic" view of life that passions and imagination cannot (*Letters*, pp. 457-59). Only when woman becomes rational, can she fulfill her social role; therefore, the ideal woman is reason personified.

---

3. II.viii.
4. Stephen, *English Thought in the Eighteenth Century*, II, 227.
5. Bate, *From Classic to Romantic*, p. 129.

But while Mr. Edgeworth swung from the extreme of Rousseau[6] to the extreme of Godwin,[7] Miss Edgeworth apparently felt uneasy about his oversimplification of human behavior. More sensitive to the nuances of personality than her father, she neither ignored her own imagination nor forgot her own emotions. Thus in the "Letters of Julia and Caroline" she only appears to illustrate the conclusions of the first two parts of the volume. Julia, whose understanding has not been cultivated, is passionate and excessively imaginative: she marries for rank, separates from her husband when she finds him "incompatible," and dies an ignoble death after a scandalous life. On the other hand, Caroline, the rationalist, finds complete fulfillment in a happy domestic life. Caroline has those ideal qualities described by the "Friend"; Julia dramatizes the fears of the "Gentleman." But the rather simple epistolary story is more than an illustration of the essays. Miss Edgeworth, for example, softened the harsh distinctions of the "Friend's" rationalism: "I . . . admire and feel enthusiasm," Caroline admits, "but I would have philosophy directed to the highest objects. I dread apathy as much as you; and I would endeavour to prevent it, not by sacrificing half my existence, but by enjoying the whole with moderation" (*Letters*, p. 469). Caroline thus represents a mean between the positions of the two earlier letter writers; through her, Miss Edgeworth admitted that the passions exist in the rational creature. To join reason and passion, rather than to wallow in passion or to exalt in cold calculation, is "a safer way to live, for this choice alone prevents the satiation of pleasure" (*Letters*, p. 471). According to Caroline (and, we may assume, Miss Edgeworth), this is neither to atrophy passion nor to give it complete sway. Reason is a part of the well-balanced personality, and it is only a part.

However sensible this opinion appears, Miss Edgeworth advanced it with reservation. She clearly showed Julia's lack of such moderation; Julia, a creature of imagination, is led from bad to worse by her uncontrollable nature. But Miss Edgeworth also showed a flaw in Caroline; her attempt to help Julia is far too limited. When Caroline advises Julia to control her passions, Julia

6. See Boyd, *Educational Theory of Jean Jacques Rousseau;* Davidson, *Rousseau and Education According to Nature;* Derathé, *Le Rationalisme de J.-J. Rousseau;* and Roddier.

7. See Fleisher, *William Godwin;* Munro, *Godwin's Moral Philosophy;* Pollin, *Education and Enlightenment in the Works of William Godwin;* and Rodway, *Godwin and the Age of Transition.*

simply cannot understand her. According to the Edgeworths, words can be understood only by the reason; the passions communicate only through action. Thus only through the satiation of experience does Julia finally understand the social code that Caroline so rationally defends. As long as reason and passion have no common ground of communication, man faces a dilemma: reason orders his existence but passion prevents the realization of that order. In *Letters for Literary Ladies*, Miss Edgeworth clearly posed this dilemma; not until *Ormond* (1817) did she resolve the extreme demands of reason and passion.

During the three years between the publications of *Letters for Literary Ladies* and *Practical Education*, Mr. Edgeworth came to accept Locke's pleasure-pain principle. As a rationalist, he sought to reduce education to a handful of self-evident laws, but children do not respond to a priori laws, however reasonable those laws may be to adults. So his experience in the nursery pushed him toward empirical ethics, and by the time he supervised Miss Edgeworth's composition of *Practical Education*, he had embraced a utilitarianism with rational overtones. As a utilitarian, he believed that nothing was good which was not useful and that nothing was useful which did not lead to the greatest (rational) happiness of society as a whole. But, to him, the greatest happiness was the negation of pain or the absence of misery.[8] Still sensitive about his failure with young Richard, he continued to damn the passions; thus he assumed that the absence of misery meant the absence of emotion. Mr. Edgeworth was not a man to do anything by halves; he could not conceive of the balance of reason and passion that his daughter suggested in the "Letters of Julia and Caroline." Rather than admit the validity of a balanced personality, he tried to reconcile gross contradictions. He needed the pleasure-pain principle to make his system practical, but he refused to acknowledge that this principle seriously contradicted his strict rationalism.

Practical Education is a key work for an analysis of Miss Edgeworth's fiction; therefore, its place in her canon must be carefully ascertained. First, we can trace a clear thematic pattern in her

8. In this Mr. Edgeworth agreed with Imlac's declaration that "human life is everywhere a state in which much is to be endured, and little to be enjoyed." Both Mr. Edgeworth and Dr. Johnson shared the thread of eighteenth-century popular thought that opposed the primitivism of Rousseau. In this sense, Mr. Edgeworth was an eighteenth-century optimist. See "Principle of Plenitude and Eighteenth-Century Optimism" in Lovejoy, *Great Chain of Being*.

fiction published between 1800 and 1809; when compared to *Practical Education*, this pattern moves steadily from the assumptions of the treatise and ultimately to a position utterly opposed to it. Second, *Essays on Professional Education* (1809) is fully consistent with *Practical Education*; therefore, the divergence that we can trace in the stories and novels cannot be attributed to Mr. Edgeworth, especially since we know that Miss Edgeworth labored to make the *Essays* a clear and logical restatement of her father's opinions. Furthermore, Mr. Edgeworth, not his daughter, was fascinated by statistics and experimental data; hence we can assume that her agreement with the assumptions of *Practical Education* would at best be superficial. Finally, if we trust the reports of her family, Miss Edgeworth portrayed herself in her fiction as a basically romantic, sensitive person. With these easily documented facts in mind, we can reduce our possibilities: either she agreed with her father at the time she composed *Practical Education* and afterwards moved from those assumptions, or she disagreed even at the time of composition and the thought of her stories and novels expresses her real beliefs. Whichever possibility we take (and both are tenable), the result is the same: the assumptions of *Practical Education* and the *Essays* are Mr. Edgeworth's, and they provide us with a standard by which we can judge Miss Edgeworth's development.

Mr. Edgeworth's thought can hardly be called coherent. For example, he overlooked basic differences between opposing schools of philosophy. Because each philosopher analyzed the human mind, their various terms were, he rashly assumed, merely a refreshing change of metaphor (*Practical Education*, II, 605-6). We can scarcely expect philosophical keenness from a man who saw little difference between Hume and Lord Kames. Furthermore, he accepted materialistic psychology, but he was not empirical enough to discard all innate ideas. Too often his philosophical jumble smacks of the Scottish Common-Sense School, but he lacked the insight of a Reid or a Stewart.[9] Unable by temperament to delve into the subtleties of philosophical speculation, he fastened on any idea that he thought would advance his basic rationalism. He failed

9. Mr. Edgeworth was familiar with these philosophers. Stewart is mentioned twice in *Letters*, and both Mr. and Miss Edgeworth looked eagerly forward to meeting him. Reid and Stewart had the same difficulties that Mr. Edgeworth encountered—they wanted to keep both reason and passion but were unwilling to allow passion a position as high as that of reason. See Jones, *Empiricism and Intuitionism in Reid's Common-Sense Philosophy.*

to see that the result was an unwieldy conglomeration of contradictions. Despite this, *Practical Education* is a pioneer work in the field of education, and like many pioneer works its merits perhaps outweigh its faults. It was the first work that attempted to reduce education to an experimental science. Whatever his shortcomings, Mr. Edgeworth had an insight into the clinical method.

Adopting the then popular materialistic psychology without considering its implications, Mr. Edgeworth believed, along with Rousseau, that the child is first a sensitive creature and later a rational being.[10] He accepted the Lockean doctrine of the *tabula rasa* and discarded the possibility of innate ideas or natural instincts as "simply the consequence of practice and industry" (*Practical Education*, I, 17). At the same time, he maintained that children have the inherent tendency to be bad; the child naturally chooses those acts that promise immediate pleasure but may result in future pain. But Mr. Edgeworth confused this inclination with the adult's imagination and consequently condemned the child's inability to foresee consequences as a *natural* evil. In short, he defined education as the subordination of the natural passions to the acquired use of reason. Reason alone, he claimed, can view the future and thereby choose the act that insures the greatest future happiness; the whole purpose of education is opposed to Rousseau's *éducation négative.*

To cultivate reason in a child, the educator must "fix the attention . . . or, in other words . . . interest [him] about those subjects to which we wish [him] to apply" (*Practical Education*, I, 57). The child by nature pursues a passionate association of thoughts, thus making the educator's role especially difficult. But failure will result in the type of permanent damage that Miss Edgeworth showed in Julia, the adult who is a creature of imagination and passion. The first step in fixing the child's attention is to teach an adequate vocabulary so that the child can express his increasing experience. By this means, attention can be fixed at any moment through a simple reference to the past.

Mr. Edgeworth also accepted Locke's notion that words and

10. Rousseau adopted this thought in *Émile*, but he misunderstood it. In *Some Thoughts Concerning Education* and *Essay on Human Understanding,* Locke assumed that reason and judgment are powers, inherently part of the human mind. Rousseau tended to make them objects that Émile acquires as he matures. Mr. Edgeworth quite openly asserted that the imagination is inherent whereas judgment is acquired.

17

things should correspond exactly. Without words, there can be no thought; without thought, no knowledge.[11] Words "are the medium through which one set of beings can convey the results of their experience and observations to another; they are in all mental processes the algebraic signs which assist us in solving the most difficult problems" (*Practical Education*, I, 61-62). But Mr. Edgeworth's lack of philosophical insight blinded him to the implications of his own borrowings. He did not understand that to a rationalist reasoning was more than "mental algebra," yet he firmly believed that as long as words were precise, the educator could control the associations between them. He accepted a notion that was at variance with his own beliefs in order to account for the development of a rational being.

Mr. Edgeworth's desire to cultivate the understanding did not end with the establishment of the blind habits of mechanical association. His goal was to guide the child into an active use of judgment, and because he usually assumed that the child has no innate ideas, he claimed that all values must be taught: "Truth is not instinctive in the mind, and the ideas of integrity, and of the advantages of reputation, must be very cautiously introduced, lest, by giving children too perfect a theory of morality before they have sufficient strength of mind to adhere to it in practice, we make them hypocrites, or else give them a fatal distrust of themselves, founded upon too early an experience of their own weakness, and too great sensibility to shame" (*Practical Education*, I, 239). In addition, he identified the hedonistic reward with the rational pleasure of virtue-for-virtue's-sake, yet common sense remained his basis for making judgments. "A gradation must however always be observed in our praise of different virtues; those that are most useful to society, as truth, justice, and humanity, must stand the highest in the scale; those that are most agreeable claim the next place" (*Practical Education*, I, 263). According to Mr. Edgeworth, the well-educated child progresses from sensation to reason, from mechanical habit to an active use of judgment, but he failed to show how the child is supposed to make such a drastic leap.

Mr. Edgeworth was in basic agreement with Richard Price's conclusion that "actions do not . . . spring exclusively from a desire of pleasure or a dread of pain, but from the mere perception of a

11. This is Locke's assumption; see *Essay*, Bk. IV.

truth."[12] He believed that the person who does not develop beyond the sensitive stage will remain a pawn of imagination, subject to whatever influence excites his passion. On this account, he had little patience with Adam Smith's "demigod within the breast" or with the "exquisite pathos" of the German Romantics. In fact, he opposed the whole conception of sympathy as a guiding power in spite of its relation to empirical associationism.[13] "Sympathy and sensibility, uninformed by reason," he said over and over, "cannot be proper guides to action" (*Practical Education*, II, 719).

This assumption presents grave difficulties. The child is first of all sensitive, not rational, but the child who is most sensitive, the one who gathers the most acute impressions from the external world, is also the one who has the greatest potential judgment. Mr. Edgeworth classified children as "saunterers" (those with no desire to learn) and "volatile geniuses" (those with uncommonly quick and vivacious perceptions). During the earliest stages of life, the "volatile genius" develops his feelings rapidly. He is the more prone to sympathize with others, and he reveals his quickness through an exquisite sensibility; he should also be able to reason with the greater acumen because he has the greater number of impressions implanted on his mind. Here Mr. Edgeworth came to an impasse. He categorically condemned sympathy and sensibility, but he still said that the child who shows these traits the most during his earliest years is the best material for the educator. The only way to guide a child from the sensitive to the rational stages was to squelch the very traits that show the greatest promise.

Thus he rode roughshod over the child's sensitivity. He believed that it is far better to crush feelings than to see a young man become a Werther. The person who shows excessive sensibility does not reason; he acts from impulse. And impulse is never good. "Let us suppose," he suggested, "a being capable of sympathy only with the best feelings of his fellow-creatures, still, without the direction of reason, he would be a nuisance in the world. . . . Such a being, no matter what his virtuous sympathies might be, must act either like a madman or a fool" (*Practical Education*, I, 266-67). To prevent this, the understanding must so firmly control the imagination that no emotion will arise without a rational choice. "The felicity of enthusiasts," he warned, "depends upon their being absolutely incapable of reasoning . . . provided they are resolute in repeating

12. Stephen, II, 11.   13. Bate, pp. 132-33.

their own train of thoughts without comparing them with that of others, they may defy the malice of wisdom, and in happy ignorance may enjoy perpetual delirium" (*Practical Education,* II, 627). But the man who participates in the world must listen to other people; hence the enthusiast invites his own misery. To talk about the merits of a free imagination is "moral insanity." "Persons who mistake in measuring their own feelings, or who neglect to compare their ideas, or to balance contending wishes, scarcely merit the name of *rational* creatures. The man, who does not deliberate, is lost" (*Practical Education,* II, 641). Only through reason can judgment be exercised; only through judgment can man act with prudence. Through the imagination man is inevitably led to the misery resulting from imprudence. Only through prudence can man be happy.

Mr. Edgeworth borrowed widely and freely and was original only in testing his principles in the nursery before announcing them to the world. This borrowing, perhaps, helped to make *Practical Education* immediately popular. People who balked at Paine and Godwin felt safe with a man who often echoed Lord Kames, Hutcheson, and Reid. Others who shunned the "dangerous" influences from Germany and France accepted echoes of Locke and Bacon. In fact, *Practical Education* found an audience in the rising industrial class that favored Pitt's repressive ministry and feared the Revolution. Nonetheless, Mr. Edgeworth's assumptions are clear despite his tendency to gather ideas at random. Originally emotional in nature, he became an out-and-out rationalist after his failure with young Richard's education. Furthermore, by comparing the "Friend's" letter and *Practical Education,* we can assert that he added the pleasure-pain associationism to a basically rational system in an endeavor to make it practical, not in an attempt to bridge opposition of reason and emotion. Finally, he debased the emotions to such an extent that he practically ignored them except insofar as they represented "bad" tendencies. These assumptions, however popular with the industrial class, are not represented in Miss Edgeworth's fiction, except in the moral tags and editorial comments that quite often detract from the fiction's structural unity; therefore, we have reason to believe that the differences which we saw between the parts of *Letters for Literary Ladies* are symptomatic of an essential difference between father and daughter.

Because Miss Edgeworth's name appeared with her father's on the title page of *Practical Education*, she was famous; for years to come her title pages were to be signed "The Author of *Practical Education*." But she was aware of the flaws in her father's thought. Mr. Edgeworth denied the validity of the question that haunted her: how can a person who is passionate and imaginative find happiness without destroying his personality? She seemed obsessed with finding an answer that would satisfy her own doubt and at the same time please her father, for when she turned to fiction, the question arose again and again. Mr. Edgeworth embraced what Lovejoy called "an ethics of prudent mediocrity"; reason was to teach man that his duty was to find his place in the social system.[14] The social code can be known, he assumed, only through reason; feelings can in no way lead to virtue, adherence to this social absolute. Miss Edgeworth wondered if the code could not also be known through sensibility. She did not question its objectivity or its universality; she merely wondered if the emotions were really as bad as her father claimed.

In other words, Mr. Edgeworth and the mass of the reading public held onto the convictions of late rationalism, but Miss Edgeworth and the men and women who would mature during the first decades of the new century looked into the vortex that would sweep the last remnants of this creed aside. In many ways, Mr. Edgeworth pushed the premises of rationalism to their logical conclusions. His religion was rational, along the lines of Priestley and Wakefield; his politics were constitutional, along the lines of Montesquieu and Ferguson; his ethics were intellectual, along the lines of Clarke, Wollaston, and Price; and his aesthetics were in the line of the worst eighteenth-century didacticism, along with those of such men as Blackmore, Akenside, and Darwin. In short, his welter of contradictions was in tune with the public that could continue to buy and seriously discuss "The Grave," "The Pleasures of Imagination," and "The Schoolmistress" and ignore "Songs of Experience," "Endymion," and "Prometheus Unbound." On the other hand, Miss Edgeworth looked forward to Scott, Turgenev, and Mark Twain. She bridged the gap between the late neo-classical favorites of her father and the Romanticism of Shelley, Byron, and Keats. Her audience of the first two decades of the nineteenth century felt comfortable in the old ways but was willing to take furtive

14. Lovejoy, p. 201.

glances forward. Like Campbell and Moore, she could lull the fears that the industrial class felt when confronted by the poets who are now viewed as the Romantic giants. But, at the same time, she had the power of subtle persuasion. She voiced the politics and ethics that made her readers happy, but she cleverly advanced the philosophical premises upon which the surging Romanticism was based. She bridged the past and the future, and she she taught what she thought was the best in both.

CHAPTER TWO

Between 1798 and 1801, Maria Edgeworth earned her reputation as a creative writer. Her father had begun cultivating her talents along this line as early as May, 1780, when he asked her to "send [him] a little tale, about the length of a 'Spectator,' upon the subject of Generosity" (Oliver, p. 65). As a result of his encouragement, her earliest stories are all didactic or, as she would have said, moral. In Ireland surrounded by her little brothers and sisters, she discovered the dearth of children's stories, there being little written expressly for children except Thomas Day's *Sandford and Merton* and a handful of tales by Mrs. Barbauld. So she became interested in didactic stories for children. The result was a series of children's books that occupied her from about 1791 till 1827. She usually wrote the first draft of a story on a slate, then read it to her brothers and sisters. If they approved, she copied it; if they didn't, she rewrote it and tried again. Her apprenticeship was truly a family affair.

This flood of children's fiction was enough to give her a lasting place in literature. *The Parent's Assistant* grew to six volumes by 1800 and was followed by *Early Lessons* (1801), *Moral Tales for Young People* (1801), *Popular Tales* (1804), *Continuation of Early Tales* (1814), *Rosamund, A Sequel to Early Lessons* (1821), *Frank, A Sequel to Frank in Early Lessons* (1822), *Harry and Lucy Continued, Being the Last Part of Early Lessons* (1825), and *Little Plays for Children* (1827). These stories and plays have a delicate brilliance that makes them classics of children's literature. Miss Edgeworth gave an unexpected life to her characters, causing the little children to emerge from her pages with a freshness seldom found in the children's literature of the last hundred years. The only flaw—if it is indeed a flaw—is the moralizing. But even moralizing does not lack charm when it is skillfully done, and Miss Edgeworth always had skill. The appeal of her stories was such that they were reprinted, both in England and America, as late as the 1890's, a remarkable longevity for this type of fiction.

Her work on this level was not an end in itself. When she first turned to adult fiction with *Castle Rackrent* (1800), her talents and her awareness of the art of the novel were already mature, and she immediately revealed herself as an artist and technician. With its rich treatment of Thady and its whimsical humor of situation, *Castle Rackrent* was Maria Edgeworth's only major work to be reprinted thus far in the 1960's, and many call it her masterpiece. But she showed her greatest talents in those books that are seldom read today, in *Belinda* and *Patronage*. *Castle Rackrent*, like her children's literature, was a step toward her more mature novels.

In her three publications of 1801, we can trace Miss Edgeworth's developing thought and art. For her youngest readers, who had advanced beyond *The Parent's Assistant*, she wrote *Early Lessons*, a primer in four sections. In one section, *Frank, A Tale*, she carefully illustrated Mr. Edgeworth's theories. This little volume is clearly didactic. There is no subtlety, no depth of character portrayal. She was attempting no more than a simple moral tale for six-year-olds. But in *Moral Tales for Young People*, a collection of stories written for teenagers, she was not interested in simple moral tales, regardless of the title. Here she debated against rationalism as she questioned motivation and narrowly limited the definition of reason. She began in this collection to develop her skill in writing on two levels, the surface of dogmatizing and the structure of doubting. The alterations of her father's thought made in *Moral Tales* were fundamental to her third 1801 publication, *Belinda*. In this novel, her first adult fiction since *Castle Rackrent*, she made one of her most subtle, and most devastating, studies of rational utilitarianism while at the same time she appeared to accept all its ramifications.

One of the most remarkable things about Miss Edgeworth's fiction is that the moral tags (whether they be chapter-headings or editorial comments) tend to agree with Mr. Edgeworth's assumptions, but the plots and characters are based on opinions which—to say the least—differ from the more outspoken tags. On this account, we are brought to the same possibilities that we discussed with reference to *Letters for Literary Ladies*: either the fiction was carelessly written, or the inconsistencies are functional.

She never openly admitted her divergence from Mr. Edgeworth's control and continued, even in the *Memoirs of Richard Lovell Edgeworth* (1820), to pay lip service to his doctrine. But she analyzed the rational premises and, when they failed to satisfy her, supplied the premises of emotionalism. The premises she introduced in lieu of the rational ones are fundamental to the symmetry of plot and to the portrayal of character. Mr. Edgeworth carefully supervised her work and was the major force that kept her writing, but she incorporated her disagreements with his philosophy so intricately into her structures that even his red pencil and scissors did not alter her meaning, however much her thought might be obscured by his desire to teach moral lessons. Thus she slowly molded the didactic novel into a radically new form. Her father's ideas everywhere struck the unsuspecting reader, but her plots, her imagery, her characterization were at odds with this surface. The resulting tension gives her mature fiction a depth that is not at all like the usual didactic novel. Had she continued to write in the vein of *Castle Rackrent*, she might have greater posthumous fame. As it was, she captivated the public and taught it to accept the Romantic premises. Thus Grace Oliver called her "emphatically a representative of the utilitarian ideas which Bentham recognized as the great movement" of the eighteenth century (pp. 535-36) and, at the same time, quoted Miss Edgeworth's remarks on the doctrine of association: "Upon its revival, this principle seems to have been over-valued, and, as Sir Walter Scott humorously observed, to have been used as 'a sort of metaphysical pick-lock.' It seems to have been forgotten, in the zeal for the power of association, that there must be something to associate with, some original capacity of feeling or pleasure, probably different in different minds" (Oliver, p. 530). In a sense, she was a master propagandist—she said what was expected from a demure young lady, but, as she said it, she swayed her readers toward the very ideas that made them afraid of the Romantic giants.

Frank is a classic example of the simple didactic story in the tradition of *Sandford and Merton*. Its sole purpose is to teach the child how to judge the proper way to act and how to avoid rash or imprudent behavior. In short, it is a narrative illustration of *Practical Education*, written for six-year-olds. A simple didactic work, it exemplifies Mr. Edgeworth's demand that "a book exhibiting instances of vice should never be given to a child who thinks and acts correctly" (*Practical Education*, I, 322). From an adult viewpoint (an adult would probably read it with the child), *Frank* also showed how Mr. Edgeworth's educational system can be put into effect.

Frank is trained by his reflective and emotionless mother who teaches him to reason and not to imagine. But his imagination is

25

not completely atrophied; his mother merely channels it entirely into scientific inquiry, the practice of judgment. In this sense, imagination is the basis of curiosity and of the use of judgment; this is a slight addition to the earlier consideration of this faculty. But overall the story is little more than a representation of the stereotyped mother and son that will show up again and again in Miss Edgeworth's more serious fiction. Because education should be practical, Frank learns such things as the production of linen from flax, the ways to mend broken china, the process of brewing beer, and the method of thatching a roof. Frank's imagination is directed away from the fanciful and to the utilitarian; hence he is obedient and prudent and happy. He is an ideal pupil of rational utilitarianism.

Frank represents the assumption that the well-educated child (the one whose education most closely resembles the doctrines of *Practical Education*) will be obedient, prudent, and useful to his society because he is a rational being, not a creature of passion. Miss Edgeworth later ridiculed this assumption.

Two of the stories in *Moral Tales* were written in the same style as *Frank*, though addressed to a slightly older audience. In "The Good French Governess" and in "The Good Aunt," the principal characters are teachers who are rational utilitarians like Frank's mother, and their pupils, like Frank, are the ideal products of rational education. But these stories are more subtle than *Frank*, for they also demonstrate the notion that to follow the rational system will result in the best possible education *with the least trouble to the educator.* Miss Edgeworth examined the implications of this notion in "The Contrast," a story in *Popular Tales*; here it merely helped her to take emphasis from the ideal pupil. In addition, Miss Edgeworth inserted premises that ultimately weakened the rational basis of her father's system. As she began to question rationalism, she contrasted the merits of the rational child and the merits of the child whose sole motivation was passion. More and more, the passionate child overshadows the rational one, and the rational child begins to show bad traits.

In his prefatory remarks to "The Good French Governess," Mr. Edgeworth called it "a lesson to teach the art of giving lessons" (*Moral Tales*, p. v). Miss Edgeworth suggested this superficial reading by centering the story around Madame de Rosier, an *émigrée* and ideal governess. Before her rational influence, Isabella

Harcourt, her oldest ward, could recite historical dates but lacked the understanding to make them meaningful; Matilda had come to believe that she had no genius because she lacked Isabella's memory; Favoretta was thoroughly spoiled; and Herbert, the youngest, was unmanageable. In short, the Harcourt nursery was a hotbed of passion and unhappiness, but the rational governess courageously tackles this challenge. She speaks to each child as though he were a rational being. Also she praises only rational and useful actions in order to form and establish pleasurable associations. When these associations become habits, the children are no longer passionate or unhappy. Isabella learns to reason; Matilda discovers that she has mathematical genius; Favoretta turns into a well-behaved little girl; and Herbert becomes manageable. On the surface, "The Good French Governess" is a simple story of reason rewarded.

Simple as it might be when compared to her later fiction, the story is complicated. Whereas *Frank* was one-sided, "The Good French Governess" contrasts the Harcourts with Miss Fanshaw, who attended a fashionable public school. Through this contrast, Miss Edgeworth emphasized the value of the private, rational education far more than she had been able to in *Frank*, where there was no background against which to judge its merits. Furthermore, she turns Miss Fanshaw's inability to comprehend the delight that Isabella and Matilda have in acquiring new knowledge into a satire on the public school. Public education teaches only one lesson well—the art of duplicity. Miss Fanshaw was proper, reserved, and quiet in public, but *"out of company*, the silent figure became talkative. The charm seemed to be broken, or rather reversed, and she began to chatter with pert incessant rapidity" (*Moral Tales*, p. 337). Such duplicity is far worse than the uncurbed passions Madame de Rosier found in the Harcourt nursery—it is reason perverted to base ends.

Maria Edgeworth also represents the bad teacher through her portrayal of Mrs. Grace, the mother's waiting-maid. Mrs. Grace creates dissension in the nursery by showing obvious partiality to Favoretta and by irrationally treating Herbert with scorn. Like the Calvinistic God, she showers her "grace" with no apparent logic. Even after Madame de Rosier brings concord, she tries to poison her mistress' mind against the rational procedure. Only when Mrs. Grace openly shows her antagonism and cruelty to Herbert, does Mrs. Harcourt take the boy out of her power. The passionate

27

mother, like Julia in *Letters for Literary Ladies*, immediately recognizes harsh actions. Thereafter, Miss Edgeworth spared no pain in degrading Mrs. Grace: she is abruptly discharged with no character reference after she is found eavesdropping, a vice that the writer strangely classified with gambling and drunkenness.

In addition, Miss Edgeworth showed that the rationality of the nursery eventually touches Mrs. Harcourt, the mother. At first, the mother "lived in a constant round of dissipation" and "had not time to cultivate her understanding, or to attend the education of her family" (*Moral Tales*, p. 284). But influenced by Madame de Rosier and by her own children, she radically changes: "The plan of education which had been traced out remained yet unfinished, and she feared, she said, that Isabella and Matilda might feel the want of their accomplished preceptress. But these fears were the best omen for her future success: a sensible mother, in whom the desire to educate her family has once been excited, and who turns the energy of her mind to this interesting subject, seizes upon every useful idea, every practical principle, with avidity, and she may trust securely to her own persevering cares. . . . The rapid improvement of Mrs. Harcourt's understanding since she had applied herself to literature, was her reward, and her excitement to fresh application. Isabella and Matilda were now of an age to be her companions, and her taste for domestic life was confirmed every day by the sweet experience of its pleasure" (*Moral Tales*, pp. 359-60). The redemption of the dissipated lady of quality, a theme fully developed in *Belinda*, illustrates the far-reaching effects of rationalism. Any person, Miss Edgeworth affirmed, will be influenced by reason, if his understanding is once awakened, because no rational being will knowingly choose misery. At this point, the writer, true to her father's assumptions, gave no leeway for honest error.

In "The Good French Governess," Miss Edgeworth showed that, if someone is not rational, he will be imprudent and that imprudence is punished by ridicule or social disgrace. Mrs. Grace was turned out with no character reference; Miss Fanshaw made a fool of herself by her imprudent behavior in the presence of Lady N—, whom she was trying to impress. On the other hand, reason leads to prudence, which, according to rationalism, is its own reward. The Harcourt children were happier because they were rational beings; Mrs. Harcourt learned the pleasures of domestic life.

Obviously Miss Edgeworth wanted to give a greater reward to the educator than to the educated: Madame de Rosier is reunited with her son whom she believed had been guillotined during the Reign of Terror. But this reunion and the later repossession of their French estates presumes a material reward that cannot be reconciled to the rational reward. The rationalist, like Frank's mother, holds that prudence needs no reward other than the happiness it brings, yet from this story on, Miss Edgeworth added a material reward (usually in the form of unexpected money) when the prudent character has successfully withstood temptation and privation. Apparently she could not conceive of a man who was both prudent and poor.

In one respect, her addition of a material reward marked one of the earliest weaknesses that she detected in rationalism: most people need a greater incentive than an abstract love of reason. Few men and no children will be virtuous for the sake of virtue, but add a few pounds or a stick of candy and virtue comes easily. In another respect, the material reward is a fitting opposite of social disgrace (especially like Mrs. Grace's) because it is social prosperity. Seldom referring to religion or to any other-worldliness, Miss Edgeworth maintained the earthliness of all punishment and reward. Thus she translated religious salvation into material prosperity. This was, of course, a comfortable pill for the rising industrial class to swallow, yet material prosperity as the ultimate reward for prudence stands diametrically opposed to the premise that prudence is its own reward. But Miss Edgeworth did not let this obscure her surface moral. At the end of the story she cleverly shifted the interest from Madame de Rosier to Mrs. Harcourt, whose reward is in line with the rational creed. This rejection of a part of that creed passed almost unnoticed. Later she so sacrificed realism and common sense that she invited Croker's charge that "we cannot reconcile ourselves to extreme improbabilities, and events barely within the verge of nature, which excite wonder instead of interest, and disgust rather than surprise."[1] But she moved very cautiously and very slowly in these early tales.

If the adoption of a material reward in "The Good French Governess" was in part symptomatic of Miss Edgeworth's dissatisfaction with rationalism, her emphasis on the disobedient child in "The Good Aunt" suggests the theme of her later fiction. Insofar

1. "Tales of Fashionable Life," p. 329.

29

as a material reward supports prudence, the role of reason is weakened. Miss Edgeworth realized that people will not cultivate their understandings unless they are promised a tangible gain, but this raised further questions. What happens if someone knows the merits of prudence but still acts imprudently? In other words, is reason really strong enough to alter established habits? If not, the assumption that reason is the sole guide to conduct must be wrong. Miss Edgeworth began to analyze this problem in "The Good Aunt."

Here her chief character is young Charles Howard, who lives with his aunt, the rational utilitarian. From the start, the story is a further development of the theme of *Frank* and "The Good French Governess." The child, however, no longer lives with his parents; Charles is an orphan. Moreover, the child's background is much more passionate; Charles' father had been killed in a duel over gambling debts.[2] The boy's education must thus overcome the influence of his earliest childhood, the time when he was the most impressionable. This gives the rational educator a greater challenge than Madame de Rosier's; however, Mrs. Howard, like Mrs. Harcourt, is willing to accept the challenge. She "had the courage to apply herself seriously to the cultivation of her understanding: she educated herself, that she might be able to fulfill the important duty of educating a child." For help she turns to Mr. Russell, a good tutor based in large part on Thomas Day's Mr. Barlow (and also on Mr. Edgeworth's own tutor), and together they mold Charles into a paragon of learning, rationality, and virtue. Again Miss Edgeworth seems to have written a simple didactic story.

But again she questioned the simple morality of the surface. She emphasized the passionate child, Augustus Holloway, by developing him into a fully rounded character. In fact, she developed him so well that he overshadows Charles Howard. Charles prudently cultivates his understanding; Augustus is blindly led into false friendships, gambling, and deceit. Charles receives a "judicious early education" from his aunt and is a brilliant pupil, but only his teachers and Oliver, his single disciple, recognize his merits. The other boys flock around Augustus, buy lottery tickets from him, and lament his losses. Charles is unpopular because he attempts to

2. To the Edgeworths few vices were more heinous than gambling and dueling. To multiply vices is one of Miss Edgeworth's rather crude ways of condemning a character.

30

win admiration only by reason and industry. Augustus wins admiration as a "man of the world" by deceiving the boys' emotions. In short, Charles stands opposed to fashion and to the social world, although he hopes that ultimately his industry will be rewarded. But Augustus stands at the top of the social ladder, the Beau Brummell of the boys' world. While Charles sinks into obscurity, Augustus commands attention. In addition, Miss Edgeworth cast doubt on the assumption that social acceptance is part of the happiness gained by the rational being. She very clearly said that popularity is a false standard of merit. She removed Charles from his peers by making him unpopular, but once he is aligned with the rational adults, he loses what interest he had. Because he is rational and always prudent, he has neither change and development nor conflict. Consequently, the entire plot centers around Augustus' mental and moral struggles. Miss Edgeworth, in other words, continually pointed at the example of the rational child, but her attention was absorbed by the passionate one. The tension and interest of the story are rooted in the troubles of Augustus, not in the felicity of Charles.

At the end of the story, Miss Edgeworth dismissed Augustus with a single sentence: "Mr. Russell was engaged to superintend the education of Holloway" (*Moral Tales*, p. 220). She had reason for such abruptness. A child, her rational father believed, should not be punished if he confesses his fault because recognition of error is tantamount to its removal (*Practical Education*, I, 249). Augustus sees his fault (indeed, he is trapped by circumstance and can do nothing else); therefore, he cannot be punished. Miss Edgeworth, then, was faithful to a rational premise. But this is not her only reason. In terms of the contrast between Howard and Augustus, this rigid adherence to a rational doctrine weakens the entire moral surface. If she wished to draw a simple contrast, she would have punished Augustus more seriously than Miss Fanshaw. After all, his imprudence brought pain and disgrace to his fellow-pupils, but Miss Fanshaw merely brought ridicule upon herself. Instead, Miss Edgeworth complicated the story by introducing a reversal in the character who ostensibly served only as a contrast to the good child. Even Augustus realizes that Mr. Russell's tutorship promises greater future rewards and that he is not really punished at all. A rigid adherence to rationalism has turned the theory against itself.

31

According to Mr. Edgeworth, a personality that is neither wholly reasonable nor wholly passionate does not and cannot exist. Passion or imagination, he claimed, results in imprudence and misery while reason alone can result in prudence and happiness; hence no one can be passionate and happy. But Miss Edgeworth portrayed a character who is passionate, happy, and prudent by using the device of making him a foreigner, a device that she often resorted to when openly contradicting rationalism. Little Oliver is "a Creole, lively, intelligent, openhearted, and affectionate in the extreme, but rather passionate in his temper, and averse to application" (*Moral Tales,* p. 158). Supposedly, he is believable because he is a foreigner and all foreigners are a little unbelievable. When he first appears in "The Good Aunt," he is Augustus' fag and is thereby linked to his master's irrationality. For example, he tolerates harsh treatment because he believes that he is stupid. Only after Charles defends his rights in a fist fight with Augustus (passion can only understand action so reason must stoop to passionate means to achieve rational ends), does he shift to the side of reason, symbolized by Charles. He becomes Charles' friend and learns from him the teachings of the good aunt and tutor. Miss Edgeworth, however, carefully emphasized that Oliver never becomes as rational as his friend. Oliver retains his passionate nature while, at the same time, he becomes prudent. Also, Miss Edgeworth made his development more credible than she had the conversions of Mrs. Harcourt and Augustus. The change is gradual and scarcely perceptible. She supported the premise that reason will win over passion if the understanding is awakened, but she gave a striking illustration of her belief that the awakening of the understanding does not mean the death of the imagination.

After "The Good Aunt," Miss Edgeworth laid aside the clearcut surface moral of her children's literature and turned toward a greater penetration into character. She had discovered that the didactic form could be molded into a vehicle that dogmatized and doubted at the same time, and she would continue to develop her skill at speaking, as it were, out of the corner of her mouth. But now her attention was drawn to another problem, one that offered ample room for developing her own opinions and for perfecting her art of ironic understatement. Hitherto, she concentrated on the teacher and on the obedient pupil, but her treatments of Augustus and Oliver posed another question: what causes a good teacher to have a disobedient pupil? In "Forester" and "Angelina" she confronted this question, and through answering it, she reached the premises that she turned to brilliant use in *Belinda*.

In his preface to *Moral Tales*, Mr. Edgeworth announced that the purpose of the volume was "to provide for young people, of a more advanced age [than the audience of *Early Lessons*], a few Tales, that shall neither dissipate the attention, nor inflame the imagination" (p. iii). Later in the same preface he added, "The Tales have been written to illustrate the opinions delivered in 'Practical Education'" (p. vi). At least in his mind, *Moral Tales* was consistent with his theory. He read only the surface moralizing and overlooked his daughter's delicately balanced plots and the probing undertones of her own opinions. Thus he missed the point of "Forester" altogether. In his heavy-handed way he told the public that it was "the picture of an eccentric character—a young man who scorns the common forms and dependencies of civilized society; and who, full of visionary schemes of benevolence and happiness [no doubt like Thomas Day, the prototype of Forester], might, by improper management, or unlucky circumstance, have become a fanatic and a criminal" (*Moral Tales*, pp. iv-v). Miss Edgeworth did create an eccentric character who is an avid nonconformist, but through an ironic understatement of situation, she twisted the story into a scorching critique of pure reason. Mr. Edgeworth was too literal-minded to understand her irony; after all, he took even Swift literally.

Forester is an imaginative and sensitive young man, a "volatile genius," who possesses such an amiable personality that his peccadillos are no more than misdirected benevolence. In fact, his misanthropy stems from a misdirected contempt for human weakness: "Young Forester was frank, brave, and generous, but he had been taught to dislike politeness so much that the common forms of society appeared to him either odious or ridiculous; his sincerity was seldom restrained by any attention to the feelings of others. . . . His attention had been early fixed upon the follies and vices of the higher classes of people; and his contempt for selfish indolence was so strongly associated with the name of gentleman, that he was disposed to choose his friends and companions from amongst his inferiors: the inequality between the rich and the poor shocked him; his temper was enthusiastic as well as benevolent; and he ardently wished to be a man, and to be at liberty to act for

33

himself, that he might reform society, or at least his own neighbour-
hood" (*Moral Tales*, p. 1). In short, he embodies the Romantic
humanitarianism that will become essential to such men as Wordsworth, Shelley, and Hunt. Like them and like Rousseau, he wants
to level social distinctions to better society. And unlike Charles
Howard, who silently accepted social hypocrisy, Forester blatantly
rejects any and all falsehood. "Those who do not respect truth in
trifles," he firmly believes, "will never respect it in matters of consequence" (*Moral Tales*, p. 24). The result of such honesty is
inevitable—he is a social outcast.

On the one hand, Miss Edgeworth contrasted Forester and Archi-
bald Mackenzie. Through her skillful balancing of character traits,
this contrast becomes the struggle between untrammeled but ignorant innocence and tainted but sophisticated cunning. Forester
is imprudent because of lofty ideals; Mackenzie is imprudent because he is selfish, cowardly, and hypocritical. In a word, Mackenzie
is an out-and-out villain. On the other hand, Miss Edgeworth contrasted Forester and Henry Campbell, the well-educated child.
Henry has the benevolence and courage of Forester as well as
genuine politeness and social cultivation. He is practical, never
carried away by imagination or enthusiasm, and completely con-
trolled by judgment. Forester is, then, poised between opposing
forces; he can move in either direction. Mr. Edgeworth or any
strict rationalist would have claimed that it was a simple either-or
choice, that Forester can either be entirely passionate and bad or be
entirely rational and good. But Maria Edgeworth did not think
that life is so simple. She showed how Forester learns rational self-
control and becomes a worthy member of society without acquiring the corruption of Mackenzie and without losing his enthusiasm.

If she were merely preaching on a rational text, Miss Edgeworth
would have made the rational Dr. Campbell play the decisive role
in Forester's education. But Forester learns only from his own experience. The rational influence of the Campbell household is not
strong enough to alter his deeply rooted habits; like Julia, he must
discover for himself whatever he learns, for precepts do him no
good. The difference between Mrs. Harcourt and Forester is significant. In Mrs. Harcourt's case, Miss Edgeworth still accepted the
notion that vice is the result of error; now her thinking had ma-
tured. Forester does not acquire prudence until enthusiasm fails to
produce its desired ends, but he does not lose his enthusiasm. Miss

Edgeworth here suggested that perhaps there is such a thing as honest error. She no longer held that virtue is a simple matter of judgment, and she doubted that reason is truly as influential as she had thought in "The Good French Governess." Thus she pushed Dr. Campbell to the background. When experience, not reason, becomes the determining factor in guiding a young man to prudence, the teacher is superfluous. The rational way to prudence becomes little more than a dream, a tea party that does not exist in the world of hard facts.

Although she showed that reason alone does not influence behavior, she did relate Dr. Campbell to Forester and Mackenzie. She contrasted the lessons that Forester learns away from the doctor and the vices pursued by Mackenzie while living under the doctor's roof. Mackenzie conceals pettiness behind an attack on an innocent woman, deceives Henry's goodness, and proves a coward when challenged to a duel. He remains in the doctor's house but learns nothing. On the other hand, Forester, separated from the doctor, reaches his conclusions without accepting his premises. Yet Miss Edgeworth's emphasis on experience is hardly complimentary. It reduces the need of an educator to mere expediency; the student will learn his lesson equally well, though with greater difficulty, from experience.

When she made material prosperity the reward for prudence, Miss Edgeworth prepared for a still further curtailment of reason. If social well-being is a reward for proper conduct, it follows that a given social order must be good. Miss Edgeworth was a member of the Irish ruling class and sympathized with the defeated French Royalists. She accepted without qualification the social order of the last half of the eighteenth century. In the narrowness of her political bias, she refused to listen to the demands for social equality that were coming from France and even from England. In "Ennui," for example, she even ridiculed men who attempted to raise their social position. Quite the contrary, she staunchly defended the status quo. She believed that the French Revolution was caused by madmen, and she never realized that her own moral philosophy was based on the same premises as the men's whose politics she so abhorred. She calmly affirmed that her society was the norm to which all prudent men must adjust, and the material prosperity she gave to her characters was firmly placed in this norm. In her ideal world, émigrés returned to their ancestral estates, the claims

35

of the Irish patriots were brushed aside with scorn, and wealth joined to a middle-class conscience formed the ideal citizen.

A rebel, like Forester, was a threat to such a society and must bend to its demands if it was to prosper; therefore, Miss Edgeworth had little patience with her character's politics. He cannot be a useful member of society until he learns that politeness is necessary, even if it means praising a young lady for talents that she does not have. Reason must adapt to society. And since reason is to further the aims of a certain society, it must, Miss Edgeworth believed, be tempered by experience lest the love of abstract theory, however rational, justify a revolution. Of course, all of this limits reason. Forester, for example, accepts society only when he finds that he cannot change it, not when reason tells him that it must remain unchanged. He first learns from experience that "Jack on his ale-house bench has as many lies as a Czar," then he abandons his hatred for gentlemen. Vice, the result of human imprudence, exists on all levels of society; hence the class which conceals it in order to live in harmony is preferable to a classless society in which all men sink to vulgarity.

In "Forester" the rational educator was pushed to the background; nevertheless, he represented certain standards of conduct that were reached through experience. Actually, the framework of the story is similar to that of "Letters of Julia and Caroline." But in "Angelina" the rational educator does not appear until *after* the main character has significantly changed. Here the author showed that experience alone can lead to prudence.

On the surface, "Angelina," like *Northanger Abbey*, is a satire of the cult of sensibility. Angelina is a young lady who "had passed her childhood with a father and mother, who cultivated her literary taste, but who neglected to cultivate her judgment" (*Moral Tales*, p. 226). Consequently, Angelina is so impressionable that, like Don Quixote, she creates a dream world of romance based on reading, then sets out into the real world to find it. Hard fact, however, slaps her back to reality every time she thinks she has found the ideal. Miss Edgeworth eked from this discrepancy between the real and the ideal one of her most delightful tales. "Angelina" is often as vibrant with rich humor as those sections of *Don Juan* in which the ideal is shattered against the hard world of facts. But Miss Edgeworth had an avowed purpose that Byron lacked. When Angelina finally can hold no longer to her tattered dreams, she turns from them with disgust, and the rational educator, Lady Frances, rushes onto the scene to "save" the unfortunate damsel. Miss Edgeworth cleverly made the story look like another illustration of *Practical Education*, but this too is merely another illusion.

Forester lived in the home of a good teacher; Angelina's guardian is a dogmatic "lady who placed her whole happiness in living in a certain circle of high company in London" (*Moral Tales*, p. 227). Like Forester, she flees from her guardian and finds herself in serious trouble before the teacher intervenes, but her flight is with different motivation. Forester foolishly thought, "I should be happy if I were a useful member of society; a gardener is a useful member of society, and I will be a gardener, and live with gardeners" (*Moral Tales*, p. 36). Angelina's imagination, completely neglected by her education, leads her to glorify the authoress of a sentimental novel. The boy wants to escape *into* the world; the girl, *from* the world. Both learn the same lesson: an unattainable sentiment is worthless. And both learn from their progressive disillusionment. But all that Angelina learns comes from her own experience; no Dr. Campbell lurks in the background.

Lady Frances, the counterpart of Dr. Campbell, meets Angelina only after she has begun to rise from her lowest ebb. But Lady Frances lacks the legal and rational powers of Dr. Campbell, who was both guardian and teacher; she is unable to reconcile Lady Diana and her ward. In this case, the first of many in the fiction of Maria Edgeworth, reason has no influence. Miss Edgeworth carefully moralized that under "the friendly and judicious care of Lady Frances" Angelina "acquired that which is more useful to the possessor than genius—common sense" (*Moral Tales*, p. 282). But she was even more careful to show that Angelina developed "good sense" before Lady Frances entered the story. It is through the frustration of having illusion thwarted by reality that Angelina discovers the disgrace to which sentimentality must inevitably lead: "Longer, much longer, Miss Hodges spoke in the most peremptory voice; but whilst she was declaiming on her favourite topic, her Angelina was 'revolving in her altered mind' the strange things which she had seen and heard in the course of the last half-hour; every thing appeared to her in a new light; when she compared the conversation and conduct of Miss Hodges with the sentimental letters of her Araminta [Miss Hodges' pen name]; when she compared Orlando in description to Orlando in reality, she could scarcely believe her senses: accustomed as she had been to elegance of manners, the vulgarity and awkwardness of Miss Hodges shocked and disgusted her beyond measure. . . . The idea of spending her life in a cottage with Mrs. Hodges Gazabo and Nat overwhelmed our heroine with the double fear of wretchedness and ridicule" (*Moral Tales*, pp. 267-68). Angelina is willing to choose any escape from this disgrace. Thus Lady Frances' entrance becomes merely expedient, necessary only for the surface moral.

By reducing the educator to a *dea ex machina*, Miss Edgeworth showed both that the result of experience, however passionate, is the same as the result of reason and that experience is a more valid guide to conduct. The passionate person—and all people, it must be remembered, are passionate by nature—will acquire through action what he cannot learn through words. Action, not words, is the basis of the experiences of Forester and Angelina, and such experience teaches the same conclusions as reason. Miss Edgeworth explored the implications of her "Letters of Julia and Caroline" and, as a result, limited the role of reason to the point that her premises completely undermine the entire school of rationalism. She showed that a person can learn to be prudent without cultivating his understanding. And even more significant, she asserted that reason was not the sole guide to prudence. Like Oliver, Forester and Angelina are neither wholly passionate nor wholly rational. They become prudent enough to be accepted by the rational educators, but they learn from actions. Miss Edgeworth proved that her own personality can—and does—exist, but in so doing, she discarded the premises of rationalism.

In the process of writing *Moral Tales*, she so perfected her art that she taught what her father wanted her to and at the same time was honest with herself. An inferior artist would have balked at the challenge; he would have done either the one or the other. Miss Edgeworth not only rose to the challenge, she turned the didactic novel into a delicate balance of dogma and doubt. She developed from the simple didactic form a technique that she would use with increasing artistry through the remainder of her career. When she turned to adult fiction with the talents that she had polished in her children's literature, the result was an astonishing array of beautifully constructed, but easily misunderstood, stories and novels.

CHAPTER THREE

A fter the attack on novel-reading in "Angelina," Mr. Edgeworth cautiously introduced *Belinda* to the public. "The following work" (he seemed to hesitate as he wrote) "is offered to the public as a Moral Tale—the author not wishing to acknowledge a Novel" (*Belinda*, I, 5). But Miss Edgeworth was no longer writing simple "moral tales" for children; *Belinda* is a highly complicated novel of manners that won even Jane Austen's critical admiration. In fact, Miss Edgeworth wrote with greater subtlety of action and better characterization than she had before, even in *Castle Rackrent*. In that novel, she experimented with the possibilities of ironic understatement in a first-person narration; now she used both ironic understatement and point of view to mold the novel of manners into a probing analysis of the breakdown of reason.

If Belinda is really the central character, Miss Edgeworth's theme is simply that the person who places reason above emotion will finally marry the most qualified suitor, From this viewpoint, *Belinda* is a typical romantic novel in which the heroine is a little more rational than usual, but this viewpoint overlooks Miss Edgeworth's artistic and intellectual development in *Moral Tales*. She had already discarded the rational premises on which *Practical Education* had been based and in their place had suggested new ones. For the rational premise that prudence is its own reward, Miss Edgeworth substituted a material reward; then she made reason subservient to the claims, however nonrational, of the society that granted the reward. As if this limiting of reason were not enough, she implied that experience was a satisfactory means to proper conduct. This was the most devastating blow that she had thus far leveled against the system of the "Friend's" letter and *Practical Education*, because it completely undermined the assumption that only reason can lead to prudence. Finally, she portrayed a character who epitomized her doubts about her father's rational utilitarianism; this character—appearing as little Oliver, Forester, or Angelina—is neither wholly rational nor wholly imaginative but is still prudent. It is a character that most reflected her own personality and one that Mr. Edgeworth said was mere fantasy. Miss Edgeworth used these new premises as the philosophical foundation

39

upon which she constructed *Belinda*. The structure of this novel, her first to deal specifically with education, is so intricately wed to her rejection of rationalism that it has often been misunderstood by persons who ignored her development in *Moral Tales*.

Miss Edgeworth was especially concerned with the education of Lady Delacour, not with the matrimonial problems of Belinda. On the one hand, she created a galaxy of characters who have little or nothing to do with Belinda's romance. These characters— Mrs. Freke, for example, or Virginia—add little interest to a heroine who is already too rational to "fall in love" without careful deliberation. On the other hand, they do add greatly to her analysis of Lady Delacour. Belinda is the catalyst for the change in the fashionable lady, but she is herself insipid. "I really was so provoked," Miss Edgeworth exclaimed when she was revising the novel in 1809, "with the cold tameness of that stick or stone Belinda, that I could have torn the pages to pieces" (Hare, I, 178). Despite this flaw, the novel remains a carefully unified whole in which the entire group of characters centers around Lady Delacour, giving her depth and developing her into a fully rounded character. In other words, Miss Edgeworth used the technique that she had learned in "The Good Aunt": what at first appears to be an overly didactic novel of manners is really one of the precursors of the psychological novel.

In broad outline, the plot is rather simple. Lady Delacour, like Mrs. Harcourt, is a fashionable woman of the world who is caught up in a constant round of amusements. When Belinda comes to her house, she attempts to sweep the young girl off her feet, but Belinda quickly discovers that her hostess is dying from a breast disease, contracted years before in—of all things—a duel. From Belinda's example, the woman of the world begins to learn patience and resignation, but her greatest change follows her separation from Belinda. Like Forester, Lady Delacour learns from experience. Meanwhile, Belinda has been courted by a Clarence Hervey, one of Lady Delacour's protégés, but he views her with distrust and she thinks him too flighty. After she befriends the Percivals, the rational utilitarians, she meets Mr. Vincent, her second suitor. Mr. Vincent is Lady Anne Percival's protégé, and she tries to convince Belinda that love is not something of the heart but something of the head. But Mr. Vincent proves to be an incurable gambler. Finally Belinda brings Lady Delacour and Lady Anne together. Lady

Delacour discovers that she is not dying, and Belinda marries her "first love," Hervey.

The structure of the novel, however, is more complex than this sketch suggests. Only the second volume takes place exclusively in the present time. The first volume is dominated by a long flashback into Lady Delacour's past, and the third volume, by an equally long one into Clarence Hervey's past. The present action is thereby balanced by what are actually the most important parts of the novel. This is significant because neither the rational utilitarian nor the titular character has any relation to the narrated events of the past.

The first flashback is a long monologue in which Lady Delacour confesses her past indiscretions to Belinda. The purpose of this confession is to create the background that permeates the novel. The coherent and full account of Lady Delacour's earlier life, for example, completely overshadows the few comments about Belinda's childhood. In addition, Miss Edgeworth introduced in the confession certain patterns of imagery and of references to events that give unity to the second and third volumes. The unifying motifs give substance to the present action by showing its causal relation to Lady Delacour's past; also they account for the inclusion of most of the characters by making Lady Delacour's experience the basis common to them all. In short, the confession acts as an overture to the novel, introducing the unifying motifs and most of the characters. From it we learn that other characters can act independently before Lady Delacour's influence, but that none can act without being altered by her in some way.

The second flashback is Clarence Hervey's "half volume" letter of confession. Lady Delacour presents the threads of the novel; Hervey ties those threads, not explained, together. The present action of the novel balances between these two long confessions, one oral and one written. But Belinda does not significantly interrupt the verbal confession and, of greater importance to Miss Edgeworth's structure, does not even read Hervey's letter. Only Lady Delacour, who both opens and closes the novel, reads the written confession.[1] Miss Edgeworth, subtly pressing Belinda to the background, can-

1. Miss Edgeworth extensively revised *Belinda* just before the 1811 edition, and this final version is reprinted in all of the collected editions of her work. At that time she altered the plot so that Belinda, as well as Lady Delacour, reads the letter.

didly placed Lady Delacour in her spotlight. Consequently, she presented the same type of surface moral that she did in her children's literature but still showed that it is based on faulty premises.

If the motifs that begin in Lady Delacour's monologue unify the novel, the image of the theater resolves the conflict and closes the book. Early, Miss Edgeworth introduced the images of the mask and the theater: Lady Delacour wears the mask of gaiety in public, dresses as the comic muse at a ball, is theatrical in her behavior toward her husband, and views her friends and enemies as actors in a play. The novel ends when the fashionable lady becomes a stage manager who describes events that lie outside the scope of the novel: "Something must be left to the imagination. Positively I will not describe wedding dresses, or a procession to church. I have no objection to saying, that the happy couples were united by the worthy Mr. Morton; that Mr. Percival gave Belinda away; and that immediately after the ceremony, he took the whole party down with him to Oakley-park . . . let me place you all in the proper attitudes for stage effect. What signifies being happy unless we appear so. . . . Clarence, you have a right to Belinda's hand, and may kiss it too—Nay, miss Portman, it is the rule of the stage. . . . Enter lord Delacour, with little Helena in his hand—Very well! a good start of surprise, my lord—Stand still, pray; you cannot be better than you are. . . . Now, lady Delacour, to show that she is reformed, comes forward to address the audience with a moral— a moral!—yes, 'Our *tale* contains a *moral*, and, no doubt,/You all have wit enough to find it out' " (*Belinda*, III, 358-60).

The structural importance of <u>Lady Delacour</u> is unmistakable. The causes of the novel's action stem from her past, and she is instrumental in bringing Hervey and Belinda together. Consistently focusing on this remarkable character, Miss Edgeworth established two opposing spheres of influence: the lady's dissipation along with Hervey's rashness and Lady Anne's rationalism—or passion and judgment. Lady Delacour's confession describes the evil of unbridled passions in society; Hervey's letter, an ineffectual attempt to thwart this evil. Together they represent the extremes of passion. Lady Anne, who acts as a fulcrum between these extremes, represents the ideals of rationalism. Her children discuss science with their father; there are no family secrets; the children are expected to reason, not to dream; and the father is a man of science who teaches through daily conversations. Her home is a picture of Edgeworthstown.

By juxtaposing these spheres, Miss Edgeworth sharpened the contrast between the behavior that resulted in misery and the doctrine that supposedly led to happiness. Lady Delacour is emotional and imaginative; Lady Anne, rational. Belinda meets Hervey at Lady Delacour's house; at Lady Anne's she meets Mr. Vincent. Lady Anne is married to Lady Delacour's first love, the memory of whom caused her dissatisfaction with her husband. Lady Delacour advocates the validity of first love, but Lady Anne attempts to convince Belinda that love is merely the result of associating the suitor with pleasurable impressions. Lady Anne supplies the excuse for Belinda's alteration from an emotional attraction to Hervey to a rational esteem for Mr. Vincent. In fact, Miss Edgeworth did not depend upon romantic tension to keep the story moving except when the rational influence is strongest. She created the paradox that, while reason and emotion are supposedly incompatible, the passions are most influential when the understanding is the sharpest.

Belinda's choice of a husband structurally establishes Miss Edgeworth's preference for certain principles. Clarence Hervey and Mr. Vincent, the protégés of the two ladies, are rival suitors. At first, Hervey is solidly within Lady Delacour's sphere of influence. He shares her passionate nature. "Clarence Hervey might have been more than a pleasant young man, if he had not been smitten with the desire of being thought superior in every thing, and of being the most admired person in all companies. He had been early flattered with the idea that he was a man of genius; and he imagined, that, as such, he was entitled to be imprudent, wild, and eccentric. He affected singularity, in order to establish his claim to genius. He had considerable literary talents, by which he was distinguished at Oxford; but he was so dreadfully afraid of passing for a pedant, that when he came into the company of the idle and the ignorant, he pretended to disdain every species of knowledge" (*Belinda*, I, 18-19).

He does not come under Lady Anne's influence until his "idle" friends refuse to save him from drowning, but even after he has met and been influenced by Lady Anne, his sole desire is to reconcile Lady Delacour and her family. He remains aligned with Lady Delacour as a creature of passion, although his experience at the

Percival's house has tempered his enthusiasm. On the other hand, Mr. Vincent is, in part, the product of a rational system of education, having been reared by Lady Anne after he left the Indies. "He used much gesture in conversation; he had not the common manners of young men who are, or who aim at being thought, fashionable, but he was perfectly at ease in company, and all that was uncommon about him appeared foreign. He had a frank ardent temper, incapable of art or dissimulation, and so unsuspicious of all mankind, that he could hardly believe falsehood existed in the world, even after he had himself been it's [sic] dupe. . . . One principle of philosophy he practically possessed in perfection; he enjoyed the present, undisturbed by any unavailing regret for the past, or troublesome solicitude about the future" (Belinda, II, 134-35). Hervey's worst fault was a juvenile attempt to rear a perfect wife; Mr. Vincent's is an insatiable desire to gamble.[2]

When Mr. Vincent fails to overcome the lure of Mrs. Luttridge's gaming tables, Belinda has no choice but to refuse his proposal. Through this failure of Lady Anne's protégé the writer showed the decline and fall of the rational ideal. Lady Anne must even apologize for her part in the affair and humbly beg Belinda's forgiveness. In other words, Miss Edgeworth turned utilitarianism on itself: if the ends are bad, how can the means be good? Later, she included her thoughts on utilitarianism in the sketchy reminiscences she dictated in her eighty-third year: "With regard to the whole system, founded on the principle of utility, it should be observed that it is more a question of words than has hitherto in the discussion been observed, even by philosophers. If each party were to define intelligibly and exactly what they mean by the word 'utility,' the dispute must come to an end. Hitherto the enemies . . . of the principle, disregarding derivation, assume that the word 'utility' can be used only in a restricted sense; as we say a chair is useful to sit upon, not considering what may be useful to human

2. According to Miss Edgeworth, "bad habits can scarcely be broken, even with the rational people, by the mere power of conviction. It was necessary, first to produce a striking effect; afterwards, by degrees, as a new generation [of tenants], better educated, and more enlightened, should arise, [Mr. Edgeworth] knew, that he might make himself better understood, and could substitute reasoning for authority" (Memoirs, II, 40). Also see her story "Tomorrow" in Popular Tales, where she fully treats this idea. In each of her accounts of rationalism after 1801 the beginning of enlightenment is based on the emotions.

happiness in general, or in giving pleasure, independently of doing service" (Oliver, p. 530).

She wanted a definition that would include the beautiful. Like John Stuart Mill, she needed more than rational utilitarianism to find happiness. When she showed the faults in Lady Anne's principles, she also showed that Lady Delacour learns to temper her behavior with prudence and that, like Angelina and Forester, she continues to be emotional and imaginative. The passionate sphere thus completely eclipses the rational. It is Lady Delacour's discovery that Hervey can honorably marry Belinda that resolves the romantic plot. Miss Edgeworth clearly placed a greater value on the impulsive Lady Delacour than on the contemplating Lady Anne. She discarded the doctrine of rational utilitarianism and, in its place, firmly established her own opinion. Yet the surface moral has not changed—Lord Byron and Madame de Staël would have been shocked to discover how close she really was to their own opinions.

Miss Edgeworth completed her analysis of the different theories of personality by contrasting two other characters, Virginia St. Pierre[3] and Helena Delacour. Helena, like Miss Edgeworth herself, attended a boarding-school until she was exposed to a rational education; Virginia received no education until Hervey brought her under the influence of Rousseau's belief that "le premier de tous les biens n'est pas l'autorité, mais la liberté." Helena is told that she must subdue her inherent passion if she wishes to live a happy life, but, like her mother, she continues to exercise her imagination. Virginia is a naturally good creature who must not be corrupted by the negative influences of society if she is to be a good wife. Helena represents a pessimistic view of human nature; judgment, a social attribute, is to control her imagination, the native attribute inherited from her mother. Virginia, on the other hand, illustrates the optimistic view of human nature; imagination, here favorably regarded, remains free from reason, the corrupting influence of society. But Helena is well-mannered, sensitive, and mature, while Virginia is naïve, sentimental, and unable to comprehend

3. Miss Edgeworth has here adopted the name of the heroine of Saint-Pierre's *Paul et Virginie* (1787), a novel in the school of Rousseau. The other part of her conception of Virginia came from her father's friend Thomas Day, who not only based *Sandford and Merton* on this premise but also attempted, as Clarence Hervey did, to rear a perfect wife. Day's attempt was a notorious failure.

reality. In addition, these children are compared to Mr. Vincent. The rational education (Mr. Vincent's) and a lack of education (Virginia's) are both inferior to the education of Helena. Certainly, Mr. Vincent's faults are more odious than those of the other characters, so the failure of a rational education appears much worse than even the failure of Rousseau's plan. Only Mr. Vincent is a dangerous hypocrite. In this regard, he is also contrasted to Lady Delacour: she appears gay and frivolous in public but reads Methodist sermons in private while he pretends to be virtuous but is actually an incurable gambler.

Miss Edgeworth, however, was not satisfied with such a black and white picture. She discredited, though with less acidity, the result of Rousseau's *éducation négative*. Hervey wants to find a pure wife and, in the heat of conviction, "read the works of Rousseau: this eloquent writer's sense made it's [*sic*] full impression upon Clarence's understanding, and his declamations produced more than their just effect upon an imagination naturally ardent. He was charmed with the picture of Sophia, when contrasted with the characters of the women of the world, with whom he had been disgusted; and he formed the romantic project of educating a wife for himself" (*Belinda*, III, 90).

But after he meets Belinda, he realizes that Virginia lacks intelligence and wit. "In comparison with Belinda, Virginia appeared to him but an insipid, though innocent child; the one he found was his equal, the other his inferiour; the one he saw could be a companion, a friend to him for life; the other would merely be his pupil, or his plaything" (*Belinda*, III, 129).

When Lady Delacour discovers that Virginia does not want to marry Hervey, she acts with reason. When Belinda marries him, Lady Anne is forced to accept passion. Miss Edgeworth wanted neither extreme; an excessively passionate person is just as bad as an excessively rational one. She sought the moderation that both her father and Rousseau lacked. Lady Delacour does not swing, like a pendulum, from one extreme to the other; she finds the single resting point where opposites are reconciled.

Lady Delacour is a brilliant portrayal of the curbing of excessive emotionalism. Guilty over Lawless' death (her husband killed him in a duel to defend her honor), she frantically tries to hide from herself beneath a mask of frivolity. Driven by her past, she craves to confess and to be forgiven, but she cannot accept Belinda as her "father confessor." A slave to the storm that brews within, she becomes a victim of jealousy and drives her only friend from her house. It is only after a short visit to Lady Anne's that she openly moves toward prudence. Still she hides in her grotesque closet, a room that calls to mind the worst tortures of the Inquisition; and the breast disease, a symbol of her inner torment, cannot be cured until she confesses and accepts penance with humility. When she finally does, the disease is no longer fatal, and she can rise above her selfish past. It is significant that she turns to Methodist sermons just before her confession and penance, for her "conversion" has all the symptoms of Wesley's "Second Birth"—except that it lacks God. Lady Delacour finds redemption through accepting prudence; neither she nor her creator was much concerned with the complications of adding religion to ethics. All that Lady Delacour needs is to curb her excesses; then she can find harmony with life. This is religion enough for her.

Miss Edgeworth never pushed Lady Delacour to an extreme position. "I am not so romantic as to imagine that I could be happy with you, or you with me," Belinda calmly and rationally refuses Mr. Vincent, "if we were in absolute want of the common comforts of life" (Belinda, III, 275-76). But Lady Delacour always acts "from the heart." Even at the end of the novel when she untangles the complications of the young lovers, she favors the union of Hervey and Belinda largely because she believes that only a passionate first love is true. The prudence that comes to her is no damper that will tame her into a Lady Anne, happily surrounded by children; Lady Delacour begins as a woman of the world and remains that way.

The relation between Lady Delacour and Belinda is reciprocal. Belinda strengthens her principles under the guidance of Lady Anne, and her patience influences Lady Delacour. On the other hand, Lady Delacour teaches Belinda to feel, an ability sadly neglected by Lady Anne. Even Hervey finally joins Rousseau's emotionalism and the Percivals' rationality. Miss Edgeworth, in other words, concluded that neither reason nor emotion can exist in a vacuum; intercourse with the world demands a coexistence that atrophies neither. A psychological balance, as developed in Hervey and Lady Delacour, is superior to the lack of balance in Lady Anne, Mr. Vincent, Mrs. Luttridge, or Mrs. Freke.

Despite the revisions in Belinda demanded by her father, Miss

47

Edgeworth used her skill and her art to probe further into human psychology than her father's facile rationalism could penetrate. Originally she planned to let Lady Delacour die. The alteration was her father's. Yet the way she constructed the final sections of the novel clearly revealed her own thought. When she contrasted Lady Delacour's passion and Lady Anne's judgment and then made Lady Delacour victorious, Miss Edgeworth was hardly in basic agreement with rationalism. But she was true to the opinions she expressed in *Moral Tales*. In a way she was like the architect of Lagado who tried to build a house by beginning with the roof: she had conclusions but lacked the premises that would give them strength. Associationism she showed to be a futile way to reach happiness, but she had no clear substitute to take its place. She suggested that the harmony of passion and judgment grew from the imagination, but she discarded Rousseau. She believed that the inherent imagination is good, but she degraded Virginia, the single character who lacked judgment. Yet her belief in the possibility was strong. She knew that imagination is a stronger incentive to prudence than reason and suspected that the imagination can make someone aware of the future. In short, she passed beyond the intellectual school of ethics and moved toward the intuitional, but she had not yet arrived.

CHAPTER FOUR

After *Belinda* Miss Edgeworth faced the challenge of developing a system as coherent as her father's, but when she further examined her opinions in *Popular Tales* (1804), she found herself in a dilemma. She wanted to say that man was innately good and that society was bad, but this opinion finally pushed her to the realization that education, whether rational or emotional, was only a futile undertaking. Then she described in *The Modern Griselda* (1805) how society corrupts the good man and portrayed the rational being as an evil, conniving woman. Of course, Mr. Edgeworth did not let this attack pass unnoticed. He so carefully supervised her next novel, *Leonora* (1806), that his ideas completely dominate it; it is the strongest invective against the imagination that appeared under his daughter's name. Then he directed her to make a further codification of his thought, the *Essays on Professional Education* (1809). But this heavy-handed treatment failed to silence her doubts. As soon as penance was complete, she restated her own opinions in *Tales of Fashionable Life*. Still, the period of forced silence taught her much. In the remainder of her works she no longer sought to embrace the intuitional school of ethics without qualification; instead, she attempted to reconcile her thought to her father's rationalism. She sought what in later writers would be called "the Victorian Compromise."

Each of the stories in *Popular Tales* was followed by the date of composition. These dates are as follows: "The Lottery" (September 1799), "Lame Jervas" (October 1799), "The Contrast" (May 1801), "The Grateful Negro" (March 1802), "The Manufacturers" (February 1803), and "To-morrow" (August 1803). If we were tracing Miss Edgeworth's development from a biographical viewpoint, the first two stories would have to precede a discussion of *Belinda* and possibly *Moral Tales*. The major difference, however, between studying the stories as they were composed and analyzing them as I have is that according to the dates of composition Miss Edgeworth's disagreements with her father's rational utilitarianism came much earlier than I have indicated. In fact, the disagreements would actually stem from the very time that she was composing *Practical Education*. However, there is no evidence to

49

show whether the published stories are identical with the form of their first composition; and, lacking such evidence, we can only analyze her thought as it appeared in the first editions rather than by attempting to recapture her actual growth.

Because *Popular Tales* was written for an audience older than that of *Moral Tales* but younger than that of *Belinda*, Miss Edgeworth had the opportunity to develop her didactic technique far beyond her earlier usage. Where she had dogmatized and doubted in *Moral Tales*, she tried now to preach two radically opposed doctrines at the same time. Earlier, the tension in her stories stemmed from her doubt; now it came from her desire to build a new buttress for the ethical conclusions. On the one hand, she openly advocated rational utilitarianism; on the other, she preached emotional intuitionalism. She frequently wrote with great skill, but was not at her best. The stories are frequently forced, and the characters wooden.

In "The Lottery," for example, she contrasted prudence and imprudence through the device she had perfected in *Belinda*. She placed her main character between two equally persuasive poles— the rash advice of Mrs. Dolly, a relative "who came to dinner," and the good example of William Deane, his friend. First, Mrs. Dolly mocks Maurice Robinson's reservations against the lottery so that, despite Deane's advice, he buys a ticket. Then, Maurice, after winning, must choose between the advice of Mrs. Dolly (to live as a gentleman) and of Deane (to invest the money and thus to prevent its rapid dissipation). Again Mrs. Dolly's sharp tongue defeats prudence. The two poles are so clearly established that the story seems to be no more than a simple illustration of bourgeois morality.

But while Miss Edgeworth traced Maurice's slow moral degeneration, she carefully described his son's faithful adherence to rational utilitarianism. For example, Mrs. Dolly, a chronic alcoholic, tempts the boy, but he rises above her corrupting influence because his mother had "pointed out to him a man with terribly swollen legs, and a red face blotched all over, lifted out of a fine coach by two footmen in fine liveries" (*Popular Tales*, p. 176). The end does not justify the means. Through this type of calculation, little George impresses a Mr. Belton, the *deus ex machina* who saves Maurice from debtor's prison. For the benefit of the surface moral, the evil influence is grotesquely punished: Mrs.

Dolly dies of a fractured skull after she falls from a horse that she was too drunk to mount. Hardly a convincing way to teach a *rational* lesson. Still, William Deane, the good influence, teaches over and over that "when a man worked for fair wages, he was sure of getting something for his pain, and with honest industry, and saving, might get rich enough in time" (*Popular Tales*, p. 192). Little George (and, for that matter, the rising industrialists) could find this moral lesson very congenial, but Miss Edgeworth was interested in much more than Macaulay's type of morality.

Maurice Robinson is neither as corrupt as his relative nor as reasonable as the industrialist. He "was an easy-tempered man, and loved quiet" (*Popular Tales*, p. 168) and succumbed to nagging female insistence. His movement to Mrs. Dolly's pole and then his final acceptance of Deane's principles supposedly reveals the alluring, but deadly, temptations of imprudence and the ultimate triumph of prudence; however, the sins of the father are visited on the child in such a way that Maurice's degeneration involves his entire family, even though little George is a rational utilitarian. The punishment for imprudence, in other words, touches even the innocent. The rational influence of a Madame de Rosier changed persons whose understandings had been awakened, but Maurice's nonrational behavior influences persons who are not at all concerned with, or involved in, the imprudent act.

If someone else's imprudence can bring punishment to a rationalist, the causal sequence set in motion by passion must be stronger than the one started by reason. In *Belinda* the gardener had not been a rational utilitarian, so this influence was not as striking. But here the influence of passionate acts is placed directly beside the influence of rational ones, and the rational influence suffers in the comparison. Actually, the surface moral of "The Lottery" is merely tacked on, very loosely, to Miss Edgeworth's more complex ideas. George's adherence to rational utilitarianism does cause his father to realize the superiority of prudence, but Miss Edgeworth has so dramatically twisted the rational premise about the influence of reason that the quick realization is scarcely believable. She *showed* how George suffers because of his father's sins, but she merely *told* that the father climbed from misery. The device that she used to advance her own ideas is simple—merely a matter of emphasis. But this simple device in her skillful hands enabled her to show that rational utilitarianism can exert its influence only when emo-

51

tionalism has run its course. Reason is ineffectual until no other course of action remains and even then only operates as a result of a mental change.

Miss Edgeworth further described the relation of prudence to an evil world in "Lame Jervas," a story about an orphan who was isolated from society until he was thirteen. "Buried underground in a mine, as I had been from my infancy," the narrator puts it, "the face of nature was totally unknown to me" (*Popular Tales*, p. 12). His education was completely neglected until he was mature; but he is noble, practical, and obedient, traits earlier attributed primarily to the Franks, Henry Campbells, and George Robinsons. Miss Edgeworth merely pursued the implications of her suspicion that society was evil. What would a person be who had grown to maturity without social intercourse? Her answer was radical (especially in the light of the lessons she supposedly taught)—she said that he will be innately good. Jervas cannot be imprudent because evil has not corrupted him. With this optimistic view of human nature (already expressed through Virginia St. Pierre), Miss Edgeworth discarded the fundamental assumption of her father's rationalism—his unequivocal condemnation of natural instincts. When she went on to equate Jervas to her earlier portraits of rational creatures, she clearly advanced a Romantic premise. Along with Wordsworth, she believed that man's natural character is sufficient unto itself. Reason may be an effective guide for someone who is already corrupted, but the innate personality would be adequate if it could be preserved from corruption.

Miss Edgeworth still did not accept Rousseau's idea of the natural man, and she carefully accounted for the difference between Virginia St. Pierre and Jervas. Virginia remains innocent but is reared as a natural woman; Jervas, who also remains innocent, studies under a rational tutor. Thus he acquires the intellectual acumen that Virginia lacks. In one sense, he is to Virginia as Émile is to Sophie; he unites an uncorrupted character and intellectual superiority, eventually becoming a wealthy but unpretentious gentleman. He calls to mind the noble savage, but he is a noble savage with a highly cultivated understanding, an acceptable member of society able to cope with its duplicity without being himself corrupted. He is better adjusted to society than Virginia, who had no contact with it.

Miss Edgeworth's unwillingness to accept the concept of the

natural man placed her in an unpleasant dilemma. She accepted her society, however corrupt it might be, as the basis for the material rewards so that, while society exerts the corrupting influence, it also rewards the person who is able to overcome corruption. Miss Edgeworth faced this dilemma without flinching. It would have been easy to advocate a revolution, as did Rousseau or Paine, but she still sought the best and most expedient way to form useful and prudent citizens. She thus de-emphasized Mr. Y—, the rational utilitarian in the story. In fact, she even implied that Jervas really educated himself. Faulty early education gave Forester and Angelina the unsound beliefs on which they attempted to act so that the role of the rational educator was primarily to counteract false assumptions. But Jervas has no unsound beliefs. The educator merely strengthens already existing patterns of behavior; he shows how prudent action, resulting from innate goodness, is also rational. In this respect, reason becomes, not a guide, but a bulwark for already existing drives.

A natural result of her consideration in these stories was her description of the vicissitudes of the material rewards in "The Contrast," where Farmer Bettesworth's poorly educated family is contrasted to Farmer Frankland's well-educated one. Miss Edgeworth concentrated on the fathers in order to advance her surface moral— "if you educate your children properly, you shall be well rewarded." But rewards and punishments are more complex than this surface moral implies. For example, Farmer Frankland loses his farm after a fire destroys his barn and he is unable to pay his rent. This is surely an undeserved punishment, especially since the fire is the result neither of his poor judgment nor of his neglect. The effect on his family of Maurice Robinson's imprudence illustrated the social dictum that "as the husband is, the wife is," but in this story the prudent man is helplessly enslaved by a causal sequence completely beyond his control. The Franklands are socially and economically disgraced; the father must go to an almshouse while his children pay his debts. Also, the material reward is earned (as it had been by William Deane) only as the direct result of individual endeavor. This is in itself a further development of the material reward as it first appeared in "The Good French Governess" or "The Good Aunt," where there was no necessary connection between endeavor and reward. In "The Contrast," no one can expect a reward for merely being good or prudent; he must actively earn it. Thus the reward is, in reality, a wage given for adapting oneself to society in such a way that the omnipresent temptations are overcome or at least subdued. Society pays a person a certain salary for furthering its aims, and this is the only reward he can anticipate.

While the Franklands are financially ruined, an unexpected windfall comes to the Bettesworths. This sudden affluence lets them assume a higher social rank, a presumption that leads to discord. Miss Edgeworth denied the freedom of social mobility; the desire to occupy a higher social position is, she now thought, no less than imprudence in the first degree. Neither the Robinsons nor the Bettesworths can become genteel merely because of money. Instead, they invite disgrace because they are utterly incapable of functioning outside their normal sphere of activities. For example, Farmer Bettesworth finally gives his daughters their shares of the money on the condition that they "never . . . trouble him any more for anything," and his sons grow more and more dishonest until, being associated with smugglers, they are implicated in a murder. The punishment of the Bettesworths is more disgraceful than the adversity of the Franklands, especially since no endeavor, according to Miss Edgeworth, can remove the stigma of public condemnation and disgrace. In this case, the awakening of the understanding is an increased awareness of disgrace; even after Farmer Bettesworth realizes the need for prudence, he cannot change. After all, a father has no second chance to educate his children.

Miss Edgeworth's next question was the logical outcome of "Lame Jervas," but it led to what, for her, was a blind alley. If man is naturally good, she asked, does he need an education so long as he lives apart from society? She answered this in one of her most unusual stories, "The Grateful Negro," where she tentatively suggested the logical outcome of her ideas. She made her noble savage, a character based on Thomas Day's "The Dying Negro," a paragon of virtue that not even her most rational character could touch and contrasted him to the corrupt, vain, selfish European who is his master. Then, she condoned the right of the slaves to rebel against their masters—obviously a complete reversal of her assumption that the status quo must be accepted as the political norm. She accepted society in "Lame Jervas" as Rousseau had in *Émile,* but here she proposed, as Rousseau did in the *Contrat Social,* that if society is remade, the individual can remain unchanged. Her reluctance to adopt the revolutionists' doctrine, however, made her treatment of the slaves' rebellion ambivalent: she lauded the principle of revolution, but she made the leader die. Revolution itself, she seemed to say, will not make a world in which the innately good man will be able to live happily; it merely changes the source of the infection without healing it. When she accepted the status quo as the source of the material rewards, she discarded the validity of revolution: either the individual must adapt to society while retaining his goodness, or he will be a victim of his own maladjustment. By establishing the innately good man in "Lame Jervas" and "The Grateful Negro," Miss Edgeworth proposed a view of man that was irreconcilable to rational utilitarianism but also unsatisfying to her sense of moderation. She knew that, only if man is by nature evil, does a rational system that attempts to curb his evil tendencies have justification, but she was not happy with the implications of her opinions. She wanted to overcome the evils of society, but she dreaded a repetition of the French Revolution.

The blind alleys of "The Grateful Negro" and "The Contrast" taught Miss Edgeworth several rather important lessons. First, she now knew that she could not, or would not, be willing to push her opinions to their logical conclusions. Second, she was forced to admit that, if her opinions were indeed valid, the ethical conclusions that she wanted to keep were illogical. Third, she saw that the only way left to provide premises to those conclusions lay in a direction hitherto untried. She was too clear-headed to stop short of an intellectually satisfying moral philosophy, but she was also too honest with herself to return to rational utilitarianism.

In "The Manufacturers," she considered for the first time the effects of education on persons who were related by family ties, the two main characters being cousins. William follows the prudent route to prosperity; Charles marries into a class so far above his own that he takes his wife's surname, Germaine. Miss Edgeworth, furthermore, concentrated on Charles' disgrace—ostracism from the class to which he aspired, loss of money, marital infidelity, and finally divorce. She hardly mentioned William, who is diligent in his work and becomes wealthy. Also, she used the device of contrast in a different way than she had before. Here the educator, not the pupil, is the fulcrum between good and evil examples, and the emphasis is practically absorbed by the bad character.

Finally, Miss Edgeworth was more consistent here than she had been in "The Lottery," where she started the line of reasoning that resulted in the dilemmas of "The Grateful Negro" and "The Contrast." The children share the misery of the parents as a direct result of their home life. This simple adjustment in her thought let Miss Edgeworth retain the material reward without much alteration although she continued to assume that it must be earned. The rational educator, a young girl of the servant class appropriately named Miss Locke, resembles Madame de Rosier, the good French governess. She is an outsider, someone who has not been influenced at all by the Germaines' imprudence. In fact, she follows Madame de Rosier's procedures so closely that she is little more than a blurred copy of the émigrée. But she earns no reward for her endeavor other than pleasure and a governess' salary.

"The Manufacturers" is not as simple as "The Good French Governess." Miss Locke does not influence the parents' change; Charles, like Forester and Angelina, learns the hard way. Ironically, Charles, not his prudent cousin, finally emerges as the character best adapted to society. "Belief, founded upon our own experience," Miss Edgeworth said in summary, "is more firm than that which we grant to the hearsay evidence of moralists; but happy those who, according to the ancient proverb, can profit by the experience of their predecessors!" Charles repented after he had been driven to the extremity of social disgrace. "His knowledge of what is called life," the author moralized, "had sufficiently convinced him that happiness is not in the gift or in the possession of those who are often, to ignorant mortals, objects of supreme admiration and envy" (*Popular Tales*, p. 316). On the other hand, William and his children are happy because they learn without personal experience, but Charles and his children have the stronger support for their actions—they have plunged to misery and realize the consequences of their acts. Society is evil, so the person who encounters it with opened eyes learns most acutely how to thwart its influence. At this stage in her development, Miss Edgeworth agreed with Milton—a cloistered virtue is not worth having.

This direction in her thought placed the educator in the position of Dr. Campbell and Lady Frances—it ultimately made him useless. In "Forester" and "Angelina," the educator had at least been expedient; in "The Manufacturers" even expediency does not justify his existence. Experience is such a superior teacher that it replaces the moralistic educator of the rationalists. But what happens if experience itself proves ineffectual? In "To-morrow" Miss Edgeworth presented a character who learns neither from action nor from words and who consequently cannot be a prudent or a happy person.

Basil's father carefully educated him, except for one mistake. When he recognized his son's quickness, he naïvely fostered the delusion that indolence is compatible with genius. Later attempting to counteract this delusion, he was a miserable failure. "What I wanted," Basil confesses, "was, not conviction of my folly, but resolution to amend" (*Popular Tales*, p. 424). The educator, then, is ineffectual. On the other hand, Basil fails to learn from experience. Every project that he begins is put off and finally left unfinished. Thus Basil is a unique character. If neither words nor actions can alter his bad habit (although he fully realizes that it is detrimental to his happiness), what separates him from those pupils who are able to learn from experience what the educator could not teach? Basil's inability to eradicate his habit is neither intellectual nor emotional. Impatience and procrastination, his faults, form a vicious circle that education and experience are unable to break, because once the circle is drawn, neither is effectual. Basil is, therefore, the rebel par excellence who cannot be reconciled to the theory of either philosophical school. Miss Edgeworth had reached, momentarily at least, a position of thoroughgoing skepticism, and she washed her hands of the entire problem of education. Yet the surface moral of the story is simply an attack on procrastination. In the first edition, the story was even divided into sections labeled with such mottoes as "Where Decision and Firmness are wanting, Genius itself is of little worth" or "The Promises of unmerited Patronage are baneful Delusions" (Slade, p. 109). Because of these mottoes, "To-morrow" has a level of ironic understatement that Miss Edgeworth was to achieve nowhere else.[1] The story in which she rejected the problems that had occupied her for the last decade seemed her most outspoken sermon

---

1. In a letter to Mrs. Barbauld of February 26, 1806, Miss Edgeworth said, "Holcroft wrote the heads of the Chapters in Popular Tales; he was employed by Johnson to correct the press. We were so much *scandalized* when we saw them that Johnson offered to cancel the whole impression. My father says that I should not enter into long explanations about trifles; but I cannot help being anxious to assure you, that those trite sentences were not written by my father and preceptor" (Le Breton, A *Memoir of Mrs. Barbauld*, pp. 112-13).

on the necessity of utilitarianism. This tour de force is truly one of her unacknowledged masterpieces.

Miss Edgeworth brought imagination and emotion to prominence in Lady Delacour. She introduced the doctrine of innate goodness in Jervas and a Negro slave and justified the role of reason as a bulwark to strengthen instinct, but in Basil she portrayed a character who defies both the rational and intuitive theories of education—a character who marks the point at which education and experience become futile. Basil is her portrait of the student who still makes educators pull their hair in desperation.

Since *Popular Tales* represents the widest divergence from the assumptions of *Practical Education* before *The Modern Griselda*, Miss Edgeworth's thought in these tales is especially important. She accepted the doctrine of the innate goodness of man and viewed society as an evil force tending always to corrupt the good man. When these notions are added to the ones we traced in *Moral Tales*, we can see that she had indeed moved far since *Letters for Literary Ladies* and *Practical Education*—so far, in fact, that she portrayed in "To-morrow" the failure of any kind of education to counteract the force of evil. Having shown that the causal sequence set in motion by actions is greater than any person whatever his education, Miss Edgeworth finally justified education by the pleasure it brought to the educator, not by the good it did for the pupil. When she wrote *The Modern Griselda*, she used these opinions in the same way that she had used the notions of *Moral Tales* for the philosophical basis of *Belinda*, but *Leonora*, written immediately after *The Modern Griselda*, utterly rejected these opinions and restated the assumptions of *Practical Education*. Either she discarded the notions that she used in her fiction between 1798 and 1806 and suddenly reverted to the very assumptions she had so utterly opposed, or Mr. Edgeworth insisted for some reason that she write *Leonora* in complete agreement with *Practical Education*. The first possibility is untenable, because the books written between 1809 and 1817 continue to develop the notions introduced in *Moral Tales*, *Popular Tales*, and *The Modern Griselda*. If she completely rejected her own intellectual development, then she had to reject her rejection—a conclusion that is obviously far-fetched. The second possibility, therefore, seems to be the simpler and more accurate. Since *Leonora* and *Essays in Professional Education* are in full agreement with *Practical Education*, it is reasonable to assume that they express Mr. Edgeworth's thought and that Mr. Edgeworth did not develop significantly during the interim between them. Furthermore, it is now reasonable to discard the conventional view of close collaboration between father and daughter as a myth probably originating, as we shall see, from Mr. Edgeworth himself. Having done this, we can give Miss Edgeworth full credit for the artistry of her works. It is also reasonable to say that *Leonora*—the only novel that we unequivocally know Mr. Edgeworth carefully revised—is the exception to Miss Edgeworth's canon. The original version of this novel is not extant; we can only make an educated guess about the changes that Mr. Edgeworth actually effected in it. Our guess, however, is based on such firm evidence from the remainder of Miss Edgeworth's works that it is sound. As we analyze *Leonora* and the *Essays*, we cannot help but to be astonished by the distance between them and *The Modern Griselda*, which is in line with the steady evolution of her thought that we have been tracing.

The Modern Griselda and *Leonora*—one written without Mr. Edgeworth's knowledge, the other composed beneath his most stringent control—are closely related. Miss Edgeworth wrote *The Modern Griselda* "in her own room, without telling any one of her occupation" (Oliver, p. 203). The first that her family heard about it was when she gave a presentation copy to her father, who appeared at first to approve of it. But the fate of *Leonora* shows that Mr. Edgeworth's reaction was more hostile than it appeared. Miss Edgeworth began this epistolary novel as an apologia to M. Edelcrantz, Swedish ambassador to Napoleon's court. M. Edelcrantz had proposed to her, and she had refused him (although her third stepmother believed that she loved him more than she would ever admit). But *Leonora* apparently underwent curious changes before it reached the publisher. After all, Mr. Edgeworth—a man who could remarry before his previous wife was cold in the grave (and do this three times) and who could invent gruesome machines to stretch his daughter—could hardly have been moved by romantic love, and Miss Edgeworth's single *affaire de cœur* seems to have been as romantic as the love affair of a sentimental novel. What he did to *Leonora* is most clearly implied in a letter he wrote to his daughter about it. The supercilious tone cannot be missed—he was taming the rebellious spirit that created *The Modern Griselda*.

"Your critic, partner, father, friend, has finished your Leonora.

59

He has cut out a few pages; one or two letters are nearly untouched; the rest are cut, scrawled, and interlined without mercy. "I make no doubt of the success of the book amongst *a certain class of readers*; PROVIDED it be reduced to one small volume, and provided it be polished *ad unguem*, so that neither flaw nor seam can be perceived by the utmost critical acumen. . . . I advise you, to revise it frequently, and look upon it as a promising infant committed to your care, which you are bound by many ties to educate, and bring out when it is fit to be presented. The design is worthy of that encouragement, which you have already received; it rests on nature, truth, sound morality, and religion; if you polish it, it will sparkle in the regions of moral fashion" (*Memoirs*, II, 353).

Mr. Edgeworth's advice mutilated *Leonora*. "It turned out to be least popular of her books. No sooner was it completed than Miss Edgeworth immediately set about to 'try and do something better'" (Slade, p. 121). *The Modern Griselda* represents what Miss Edgeworth could do apart from her father; *Leonora* is an example of his direct supervision.

In *The Modern Griselda* Miss Edgeworth illustrated the notion that "had Chaucer lived in our enlightened times, he would doubtless have drawn a very different character" of Griselda (p. 55). Such a notion is, of course, a natural outcome of the opinions she advanced in *Popular Tales*. If society corrupts people today, could a person who lived several hundred years ago have remained good? This is merely another approach to the questions of "The Grateful Negro"; the past must have been less corrupt than the present because society was not as powerful. In order to establish this contrast between the past and the present, Miss Edgeworth juxtaposed the Patient Griselda of the *Clerk's Tale* and Griselda Bolingbroke, a corrupt "lady" of the early nineteenth century, but she wrote with more than a simple contrast in mind. After all, the Patient Griselda was married to a man who attempted every possible means to break her spirit, but, ironically, Griselda Bolingbroke is married to a man too weak to withstand her wiles. Griselda Bolingbroke is as sadistic a *femme fatale* as any of the decadent heroines that Mario Praz studied in *The Romantic Agony*.

The underlying premise of the novel is optimistic. That is, it is as optimistic as any primitivism can be; the characters are corrupted by their contact with society, not depraved by nature.

Griselda also attempts to corrupt others. It is almost as though Miss Edgeworth placed people in two camps—those who were innocent and nonconforming and others who were corrupt and conforming. For example, Mr. Bolingbroke, a romantic sentimentalist, is innocent until he marries, but his wife desires so much "to han the governance of hous and land,/ And of his tonge and his hand also" that she will go to any extreme. A cunning rationalist, she turns her husband's sentimentality into her strongest weapon. Moreover, Miss Edgeworth now associated sentimentality and innocence. She merely reversed the value judgments of rationalism by saying that sentiment was good and reason evil. Sentimentality, tenderness, sympathy were innate; reason, judgment, calculation came from the society that despised any emotional feeling. Thus, even though the underlying premise is optimistic, Miss Edgeworth had little hope for society or, for that matter, for the plight of modern man.

Nevertheless, the innocent pawn does emerge victoriously. In fact, *The Modern Griselda* is one of the earliest novels to analyze the events that end in a fully justified separation of husband and wife. The separation is more than merely justified; it is the only way the single good partner can remain uncorrupted. While the entire blame is placed on the wife, Mr. Bolingbroke is an entirely sympathetic character. He has faults, but his greatest is merely that he loves too much to perceive his wife's manipulation of his feelings. When she drives off in her carriage at the end of the novel, he is no longer innocent, but he has not been corrupted enough to conform to society.

As if this juxtaposition of good and evil was not dramatic enough to emphasize her opinion of rationalism, Miss Edgeworth also contrasted Griselda and Emma Granby, an obedient wife who by relinquishing her claims to superiority finds such power over her husband that he seeks only her happiness. The disgraceful behavior of the conniving wife is fully seen when she invites Emma to a reading of the *Clerk's Tale*. She anticipates that her guests will "laugh at *the pattern wife, the original Griselda revived*" (*Griselda*, p. 43). The irony of this scene can hardly be missed. The namesake has none of the qualities of the original, but the woman she mocks is as patient a wife as anyone could desire. For example, Emma's patience at the party "really placed [her] understanding, manners, and temper, in a most advantageous and amiable light"

(*Griselda*, p. 56). Griselda reveals only her own malicious personality; she ridicules and then slanders the uncorrupted woman whose goodness puts her in a bad light.

Miss Edgeworth was no more specifically concerned with education here than she had been in *Castle Rackrent*, yet both novels, written without her father's knowledge, imply the superiority of passionate to rational behavior. Thady's calculating son, not the simple-minded landlord, was the villain of *Castle Rackrent*; similarly, the calculating wife is the villain of *The Modern Griselda*. Also, there is an affinity between *The Modern Griselda* and *Belinda*. The passionate characters in both are contrasted to the rational and are held in greater esteem. Griselda, like Lady Delacour, seeks to control her husband, but she pushes too far and, unlike Lady Delacour, separates from him. In addition, Belinda and the Percivals had influenced Lady Delacour, but Griselda is too corrupt to consider the prudent examples constantly held before her. Also the prudent educator is thwarted in both novels. In *Belinda* Lady Delacour was ultimately superior to Lady Anne; in *The Modern Griselda* there is no communication between Emma and Griselda. The Granbys' interference does lead indirectly to the separation, because they point out to Mr. Bolingbroke the gravity of his situation. But they wanted to bring the husband and wife together again. Finally, reason plays a much different role than it had in Belinda. There, it carried Lady Delacour toward domestic happiness; here, it pushes Griselda toward a separation from her husband.

In contrast, the epistolary novel *Leonora* is the portrayal of the seduction of the rational Leonora's emotional husband by the excessively sentimental Olivia and of the way Leonora, by remaining faithful to her rationalism, wins him back. Only the complete absence of Miss Edgeworth's own opinions parallels the lack of spontaneity and of convincing character portrayal. There is no deviation from Mr. Edgeworth's assumptions. All the value judgments of *The Modern Griselda* are thrown aside, and characters are either entirely virtuous or depraved beyond the hope of redemption. From her first letter, Olivia is a bad woman because, and simply because, she is sentimental; her only development is to become worse. Likewise, Leonora is good, never stepping from her inhuman rationalism even when a mere sign of affection might win her husband back.

Why Mr. Edgeworth's assumptions so utterly dominate *Leonora* is a curious question. Miss Edgeworth published *Griselda* before he knew anything about it, but that would hardly account for his sudden repression of her opinions. After all, she published *Castle Rackrent* without his knowledge, and he did not force his assumptions onto *Moral Tales*. *The Modern Griselda* and *Castle Rackrent* have much in common despite appearances. But of all similarities the most important—and also the most obvious once it is recognized—is the lack of the little moral tags and editorial comments. Neither novel uses the technique of doubting and dogmatizing that Miss Edgeworth perfected in *Moral* and *Popular Tales*. In fact, the lack of such double intent makes *The Modern Griselda* her most outspoken attack on rational utilitarianism, for there is nothing between her opinions and the reader. We saw examples of Mr. Edgeworth's lack of philosophical keenness in *Practical Education*; this blindness was perhaps the reason he approached his daughter's fiction with such naïveté. As long as there were moral tags to delude him, he believed that she completely agreed with him, but when he read a novel that lacked such tags, he clearly saw the "dangerous" propensities that he had tried to repress when she was still a teenager. It took, in other words, no depth of insight or awareness of fictive structure to see that *The Modern Griselda* attacked the very assumptions he had staked his life on. This sudden realization—indeed shock—combined with the fact that she had published the book surreptitiously must have put him on the defensive, so much so, in fact, that he forcibly silenced her doubts between 1806 and 1809.

In *Belinda* the emphasis fell on Lady Delacour while Belinda faded into the background, and in *Moral Tales* Forester and Angelina took emphasis from their educators. But in *Leonora,* even though Leonora herself remains always in the spotlight, she is not as strongly developed as Dr. Campbell or Lady Frances. She is interesting only to the extent that her rationalism leads to misery. Because Olivia is everywhere in an unfavorable light, Leonora is forced upon the reader. Perhaps, this prominence accounts for her glaring faults: she is so clearly delineated that otherwise neglected traits are strikingly visible. She even becomes a little ridiculous (obviously unintentionally) when she refuses to show feeling for her husband. In short, she is altogether too cold and too calculating to be attractive even as a paragon of morality.

The treatment of German Romanticism is indicative of the moral tone of *Leonora* and of its unqualified rejection of sentimentality.[2] "To the bold genius and exquisite pathos of some German novelists," Olivia freely confesses, "I hold myself indebted for my largest portion of ideal bliss" (*Leonora*, I, 8). But this admiration has so blinded her to reality that she lives in a dream world: "Upon recollection, in my favourite 'Sorrows of Werter,' the heroine is represented cutting bread and butter for a groupe [*sic*] of children; I admire this simplicity in Goethe, 'tis one of the secrets by which he touches the heart. Simplicity is delightful by way of variety, but always simplicity is worse than *toujours perdrix*. Children in a novel or a drama are charming little creatures: but in real life they are often insufferable plagues" (*Leonora*, I, 73-74).

Leonora explains that before Olivia "married, a strict injunction was laid upon her, not to read any book that was called a novel: this raised in her mind a sort of perverse curiosity" (*Leonora*, I, 51-52). Both *Letters for Literary Ladies* and *Practical Education* forbade the reading of novels, but curiosity was channeled into specific scientific pursuits; Olivia's curiosity was allowed to run amuck in imaginative novels after she married. The morality of *Leonora* is free from the complexity of Miss Edgeworth's usual fiction. If a girl reads a German novel, it can be summed up, she will grow into a seductress. The outspoken promoter of this sort of rationalism is the Duchess, who minces no words in condemning sentimentalism: "These orators seem as if they had been fed by Satan to plead the cause of Vice; and as if possessed by the evil spirit, they speak with a vehemence which carries away their auditors, or with a subtlety which deludes their better judgment. They put extreme cases, in which virtue may become vice, or vice virtue: they exhibit criminal passions in constant connexion with the most exalted, the most amiable virtues; thus making use of the best feelings of human nature for the worst purposes, they engage pity or admiration perpetually on the side of guilt. Eternally talking of philosophy and philanthropy, they only borrow the terms to perplex the ignorant and seduce the imaginative" (*Leonora*, I, 21-22).

In addition, the Duchess (clearly a spokesman for the rational-

2. In the light of this attack on German Romanticism, it is interesting that on January 28, 1805, Mrs. Barbauld drew Miss Edgeworth's attention to William Taylor's translation of Bürger's *Lenore*. As Griselda Bolingbroke is a reversal of Chaucer's patient wife, Leonora is a reversal of the romantic heroine of this ballad.

ism of Edgeworthstown) blames novel reading for the excesses of Olivia and of all young women who are carried away by passions: "The mental intemperance that they indulge in promiscuous novel-reading," she dogmatizes, "destroys all vigour and clearness of judgment, every thing dances in the varying medium of their imagination" (*Leonora*, I, 43). Unlike Lady Anne, the Duchess is a rationalist who is always correct, clearly stating the very doctrine that Miss Edgeworth had found unsatisfying.

This condemnation of novels is paralleled by the demand to repress all emotions. Such repression can be carried to an unhealthy extreme, and in *Leonora* it is. For example, Leonora's husband, who has a passionate nature, is tempted by the uninhibited Olivia only after his wife shows no emotional attachment whatever to him; the only argument Leonora advances (other than the esteem which she will not show) is reason. But the passionate person cannot understand reason; the husband is repelled until he is bedridden with a nearly fatal disease, at which time Leonora can show her cold affection by nursing him back to health. After this, his understanding is awakened, and he too can see the value of a rational life. But, by then, his emotions have been stifled.

By manipulating the plot to contrive this "happy ending," Miss Edgeworth completely sacrificed verisimilitude with the unavoidable insinuation that rational utilitarianism is practical only if reality is ignored. The artificiality of the final reconciliation, the incredibility of the husband's reversal, and the lack of any insight into Leonora's character border on the ridiculous. Miss Edgeworth was usually too clear-headed to descend to bathos; the plots of some of her children's stories, for example, might be far-fetched but never ridiculous. Perhaps this unexpected bathos is a further example of the difficulty she found in her father's assumptions; perhaps she even retained enough of her own opinions to make *Leonora* an extremely clever—and subtle—critique of the unreality of rational utilitarianism. But these possibilities make the little novel far more sophisticated than it really is; Miss Edgeworth simply was not as skillful or as artistic as she had been in *Belinda* or the children's tales. From all appearances she sincerely attempted to illustrate her father's assumptions; if the novel is unrealistic, the fault lies with the assumptions, not with the endeavor of the author to write with double intention. This lack of verisimilitude may well account for the fact that while *Popular Tales*, *Belinda*, and *The Modern Gri-*

selda went into second editions within a year of their original publications, *Leonora* waited nine years.

Miss Edgeworth, in other words, followed her father's doctrine
to the letter in this novel, but she made it look as untenable as
Lord Monboddo's extravaganzas. Where *The Modern Griselda* is
realistic, *Leonora* implicitly contradicts the very doctrine it attempts to propagate. After all, if rationalism needs a make-believe
world to be an active force in human affairs, it is no more than a
fantasy. When Mr. Edgeworth attempted to make *Leonora* "sparkle
in the regions of moral fashion," he forced his daughter to ignore
the very opinions that might have given morality a realistic basis.
As it was, he ended up making a fool of the rational utilitarian.

After the publication of *Leonora*, Miss Edgeworth was called
upon to make a further codification of her father's thought. *Essays
on Professional Education*, her next work, was a treatise on the
ways to educate children who had successfully passed through
Practical Education. The book was the result of Mr. Edgeworth's
ideas although it lacks the experimental foundation of the earlier
book. Miss Edgeworth labored through its composition, doing much
of the research herself, but only her father's name appeared on the
title page. "Probably it was thought," Grace Oliver conjectured,
"that it would not be considered as valuable by the public if the
hand of a woman was detected in its composition" (p. 225). Perhaps it might be just as sensible to say that she did not want to
sign the work, for the treatise is little more than a watered down
repetition of *Practical Education*. In fact, Miss Edgeworth was so
aware of her father's intellectual narrowness that she feared the
public reception of the *Essays*: "I am well repaid for all the labour
this copying and correcting has cost me, by seeing that my father
is pleased with it and thinks it a proof of affection and gratitude.
I cannot help, however, looking forward to its publication with an
anxiety and apprehension I never felt before for I consider my
father's credit is at stake" (Slade, p. 123).

If she had not questioned her father's assumptions and found
them wanting, she would have little reason for this concern; she
knew the limits of rational utilitarianism and feared that the public
might attack him, for, however much she disagreed with his assumptions, she loved him and wanted others to respect him. Perhaps her anxiety may account for the fact that the two outstand-
ing additions—an extended discussion of religion and religious

training and the acceptance of the role of the imagination in the training of a child intended for the military—are concessions to public opinion.

Early in the treatise, Mr. Edgeworth (I will credit him with the ideas since he was obviously the mastermind behind the composition) assumed that "nothing . . . should prevent a wise parent from determining early on the profession of his child" (*Essays*, p. 5). Still adhering to associationism, he denied the doctrine of natural genius. For example, a child, after his parents have chosen his future profession, should be allowed to associate only good ideas with their choice; consequently, he will prefer their choice to his own (*Essays*, p. 14). But "parents should observe," Mr. Edgeworth now admitted, "that the power of education, great as it is, cannot, even in the most judicious hands, and with the most vigilant care, command all those external, accidental circumstances, which, influencing early associations, produce taste and predilection for certain pursuits" (*Essays*, p. 22). This admission allowed him to account for the boy who refuses to bend to his parents' will. In addition, Mr. Edgeworth warned the parent to avoid at all cost the "impracticability and romance of Rousseau's general system of education" (*Essays*, p. 130). The parents' will alone should determine the child's actions. Rationalism thus becomes a calculated determination in which the parent plays the role of God.

Parents can measure the capacity of their children and determine the most fitting profession for each if they act from the dictates of reason, which foresee the effects of present causes, and seek present causes for desired later effects. The child, predominantly "enthusiastic" or highly emotional, is passive when he receives this stimulus. According to Mr. Edgeworth, the child cannot view himself with the detachment of his parents and cannot judge the effects of present actions because he lacks reason. But the child does have the ability to select from circumstances and to combine these simple impressions into complex thoughts. This ability he called "imagination," and in this role imagination can be beneficial if it furthers the cultivation of the understanding. Since the parent uses imagination in order to reach the preconceived goal, he must keep it in reasonable control. If it is allowed to run free, the parents will lose the ability to guide its selection or combination. Thus while he saw that imagination is essential to the rational development of the child, Mr. Edgeworth warned

67

against allowing too much free exercise and suggested that, when it is properly used, it will be totally subordinated to reason. He did not suggest a mixture of reason and emotion; the desideratum of his theory is the cultivation of reason at the expense of enthusiasm or emotion.

But imagination has a greater role than this. Mr. Edgeworth—perhaps more as a utilitarian than as a rationalist—accepted with limitations the romantic imagination that he had unconditionally anathematized in *Practical Education*. If, he now reasoned, imagination leads people away from reality, someone who exercises it will be unhappy, because illusion cannot be as pleasurable as reality. But if the dream world can make a person happier when he faces reality, the dream world, and hence the imagination that created it, has a utilitarian function. This use of the imagination is precisely what he proposed in his chapter on military education: "The first books [to be read by the child intended for the army or navy] should be such as are calculated to rouse in his young mind the notions of honour, and the feelings of emulation. In his education it must be the object to excite enthusiasm, not to subject him at an early age to the nice calculations of *prudence*. Consequently a species of reading, which may be disapproved of for other pupils, should be recommended to the young soldier. His imagination should be exalted by the adventurous and the marvellous. Stories of giants, and genii, and knights and tournaments, and 'pictured tales of vast heroic deeds,' should feed his fancy" (*Essays*, p. 137).

In *Practical Education*, Mr. Edgeworth had admitted that "this species of reading should not early be chosen for boys of an enterprising temper, unless they are intended for a seafaring life, or for the army. The taste for adventure is absolutely incompatible with the sober perseverance necessary to success in any other liberal profession" (I, 336). Now he expanded this notion into a major idea, an idea that is hardly in tune with the rationalism of the rest of the treatise.

Mr. Edgeworth had forced his daughter to do penance for her condemnation of rationalism in *The Modern Griselda*, but he too had moved from the narrow ideas of *Letters for Literary Ladies*. Still his intellectual development advanced slower than his daughter's. In fact, her thoughts were so far in advance of his that his prefaces to her novels and stories reveal only his inability to read fiction. Approaching her works with preconceived ideas, he saw only the intrusive moral tags. He based his opinions on these tags and overlooked her delicately balanced structures until she wrote a straightforward attack on rationalism. When he saw this, he attempted to silence her doubts, but her probing mind was not that easily silenced.

CHAPTER FIVE

Maria Edgeworth could never idly fold her hands in her lap and watch the world go by. She was constantly busy, if not using her hands to knit clothes for her large number of nieces and nephews, then using her mind in thinking. Thus the time that she spent in the laborious tasks of revising *Leonora* and compiling *Essays on Professional Education* was not altogether wasted. She continued to probe the problems that had led to "To-morrow," and to search for a way to be honest with herself and still please her father. The period of forced silence was actually beneficial. It was the turning point of her career. In what she wrote during the remainder of her life, she still used the didactic form to reconcile her doubts and her father's dogma. She might not have been as productive in terms of quantity as she had earlier been, but she certainly was superior as a technician and artist.

Her first books after *Essays on Professional Education* were the First (1809) and the Second (1812) Series of *Tales of Fashionable Life*. As was his usual practice, Mr. Edgeworth wrote a preface for the earlier collection. Usually he merely pointed out the moral lesson that he supposed the work contained, but in this preface he did more. He misleadingly asserted that his daughter promoted "by all her writing, the progress of education, from the cradle to the grave. . . . In 'The Parent's Assistant,' in 'Moral' and in 'Popular Tales,' it was my daughter's aim to exemplify the principles contained in 'Practical Education.' In these volumes, and others which are to follow, she endeavours to disseminate, in a familiar form, some of the ideas that are unfolded in 'Essays on Professional Education'" (*Fashionable Life*, I, v-vi). An obvious overstatement. Then, he gave the dates on which the stories were written, supposedly to "show, that they have not been hastily intruded upon the reader" (*Fashionable Life*, I, viii). The combination of these assertions is interesting. Miss Edgeworth wrote *Essays on Professional Education* during 1807 and 1808, but only one story was dated after 1808. How could she endeavor to "disseminate" ideas long before they were conceived? Either the ideas of the treatise were germane to her thought as early as 1802 (the date affixed to "Almeria" and "The Dun"), or she significantly revised the stories in 1808 and 1809. The latter, while possible, suggests that Mr. Edgeworth's assertion is a conscious falsehood. But the former is equally questionable. In a letter of January 23, 1808, Miss Edgeworth described how much trouble she was having with some of the essays; moreover, she said that she sent the manuscript to authorities in different fields for additional help. It is, therefore, improbable that ideas germinated and codified with such difficulty in 1807 and 1808 were influential in 1802.

There is only one way to read Mr. Edgeworth's preface. He forced upon his daughter's fiction a didactic intention that was alien to it. Subsequent readers, approaching the stories from his view, have overlooked Miss Edgeworth's own thought. They have ignored her structures and emphasized the very moral tags that misled her father. Mr. Edgeworth could not see beyond superficial details. He failed—and he made others fail—to see that Miss Edgeworth was not writing simple moral sermons. If we closely examine one story from each of the series, we can readily see exactly what Miss Edgeworth was doing in these misunderstood tales.

Of "Madame de Fleury," a story in the First Series (1809), Mr. Edgeworth wrote: "*Madame de Fleury*—points out some of the means, which may be employed by the rich for the real advantage of the poor. The story shows, that sowing gold does not always produce a golden harvest; but that knowledge and virtue, when early implanted in the human breast, seldom fail to make ample returns of prudence and felicity" (*Fashionable Life*, I, vii). The story does suggest this superficial moral—but only through the intrusive moral tags. A closer look at the work shows that Miss Edgeworth was only incidentally concerned with this surface moral.

The setting of "Madame de Fleury" is Paris at the outbreak of the Revolution. Miss Edgeworth had completely discarded the revolutionists' doctrine that she toyed with in "The Grateful Negro."[1] If the rich were benevolent to the poor, she now argued, the atrocities of a French Revolution could have been prevented and Paris could have escaped further misery. Instead, a handful of brutal madmen unleashed the destructive force, killing rich and poor

1. According to the date that follows "Madame de Fleury," it was composed in 1802, the same year as "The Grateful Negro." I presume that it followed the other story, but since there is no evidence of what the original story was like (if it was different), its appearance following *Leonora* and *Essays on Professional Education* supports my view that Miss Edgeworth returned to her doubts after the period of forced silence was ended.

71

without discrimination. But she had more than hindsight. Although the setting is French, the characters are very English. What might have saved the French could still, she thought, save the English. She wanted a benevolent aristocracy to calm the murmuring laboring class of England but still preserve the Constitution.

Education alone can strengthen the lower classes against misery, but education—and here Miss Edgeworth clearly showed her narrow political bias—is practical only for the laborers who are faithful to the *ancien régime*. Since Madame de Fleury, a recreation of Madame de Rosier, escapes the guillotine and finally repossesses her estates, Mr. Edgeworth seems to have had ample grounds for his prefatory remarks. But Madame de Fleury is not the educator. She just finances the undertaking, being very careful in her choice of pupils not to admit any child with radical leanings. The educator is Sister Frances, a nun whom Madame de Fleury rescued from the hands of the revolutionists. The aristocratic lady does not otherwise infringe upon the process of education. She merely saves her own neck by indoctrinating with rational utilitarianism the poor who under the nun learn that it is not to their benefit to guillotine the rich. Education, in other words, is little more than an instrument of the rich for the preservation of the status quo.

Miss Edgeworth obviously doubted the value of this type of education. Sister Frances, for example, earns a strange reward for her troubles: "Two of the youngest of the children, who had formerly been placed under her care, and who were not yet able to earn their own subsistence, she kept with her, and in the last days of her life she continued her instructions to them with the fond solicitude of a parent. Her father confessor, an excellent man, who never even in these dangerous times shrunk from his duty, came to attend Sister Frances in her last moments, and relieved her mind from all anxiety, by promising to place the two little children with the abbess of her convent, who would to the utmost of her power protect and provide for them suitably. Satisfied by this promise, the good Sister Frances smiled upon Victoire, who stood beside the bed, and with that smile upon her countenance expired" (*Fashionable Life*, II, 297-98). This is not the "ample returns" that Mr. Edgeworth recognized. Yet Sister Frances did join the religious and the rational roles as well as could be expected, and she does have the reward of as painless a death as David Hume's.

While the nun dies and hence does not see Paris under Robespierre and Danton, Madame de Fleury, who supposedly wins material prosperity, returns to Paris while it is still torn by factions. She really has no reward either from a traditional Christian or from a conservative English viewpoint. The circumstances into which Paris fell with the increasing power of Napoleon ironically undermine her final confidence: "'No gratitude in human nature! No gratitude in the lower classes of the people!' cried she: 'How much those are mistaken who think so!'" (*Fashionable Life*, II, 328). In 1809 these glowing words would have immediately suggested the blindness of the speaker. She alone did not understand that mankind is deluded by appearances of good and that evil will corrupt as Napoleons continue to rise. As early as 1802, Miss Edgeworth had forcibly learned that the evil in France was not over, and when she wrote the story, one of her brothers was still held in a French detention camp. Thus the rewards of "Madame de Fleury" are little more than delusions. Miss Edgeworth might approve of educating the poor, but she hardly condoned the indoctrination with rational utilitarianism.

By analyzing the pupils in Madame de Fleury's school, perhaps, we can come even closer to Miss Edgeworth's opinions. Victoire is the obedient pupil who is contrasted to her cousin Manon. Victoire's education teaches her "by slow and sure degrees, to be a good, useful, and happy member of society." It, therefore, ignores imagination (poetry, for example, is frowned upon) and the social graces (dancing and music are banned from the school). The girls are trained to be "shop-girls, mantua-makers, work-women, and servants of different sorts. Consequently they were instructed in things which would be most necessary and useful to young women in their rank of life" (*Fashionable Life*, II, 234-35). Like the National Society for Promoting the Education of the Poor in the Principles of the Established Church, Madame de Fleury has no desire to level class distinctions; she seeks to teach the members of the lower class to accept their status and to be industrious. Through the nun the pupils learn little more than stoic acceptance which atrophies their imaginations. This is a way to preserve the status quo, and Victoire is properly obedient. But if—the question lingers in the background—the status quo has already been disrupted, is this a very practical approach? From Madame de Fleury's reward we gather that Miss Edgeworth apparently had reservations.

There is a positive side to her opinions in "Madame de Fleury."

The moral problem, on one level, can be formulated in a simple definition: prudence is the acceptance and fulfillment of one's social position, and imprudence is the attempt to disregard the status quo. In other words, there are two kinds of society: one is static (a rigid society, justified by an absolutism in religion, politics, and philosophy); the other is dynamic (social mobility, supported by a relativism in religion, politics, and philosophy). Like many of the clearest minds of the nineteenth century, Miss Edgeworth wanted to have the best in both, but she found herself in a maze of self-contradictory premises. For example, she was never willing to discard the absolute of politics, even though she quite readily accepted the relativity of moral philosophy; therefore, in *Castle Rackrent* Thady disclaims his son for aspiring to a higher class and also overlooks his landlord's drunkenness on the ground that an aristocrat needs some foibles. Nevertheless, in "Madame de Fleury" the clash of the static and dynamic societies created a tension that she was unable to resolve. If the goal of education is merely to maintain the existing social order, the lower class must be taught to accept its lot. But the society of "Madame de Fleury" is no longer static, and the material rewards that seemed to work so well in the *ancien régime* are no longer applicable. In a dynamic society the prudence of the old way of life becomes intolerance. Miss Edgeworth thus showed that just as Madame de Fleury's material reward is actually punishment, Victoire's education is as wrong in one way as Manon's is in another. Neither the route of the revolutionists nor the path of the conservative rationalists is without fault. This much Miss Edgeworth clearly saw, and she now fully realized that the harmonious mixture of imagination and reason that she mentioned in *Belinda* was the most acceptable guide to happiness. This mixture appeared in Sister Frances. As a Catholic nun she represents the emotional and imaginative framework of the Church, but as an educator she embodies the rationality of Edgeworthstown. She earns a peaceful death as a result of her emotional propensity, and she avoids the corruption of Parisian life while she participates in it as a rational utilitarian. In this respect, Sister Frances, the only character who remains aloof from material rewards, is an example of conduct that is neither cloistered nor profligate. Through her, Miss Edgeworth demonstrated the harmonious mixture that she found in herself, but she had not worked out the blatant contradictions of this opinion.

In "Vivian," a story in the Second Series of *Tales of Fashionable Life* (1812), Miss Edgeworth was concerned with a young man, similar to Basil in "To-morrow," whose lack of determination and steadfastness of purpose eventually cause his death. In the other tales of this series, "Emilie de Coulanges" and the more famous *The Absentee*, the deliberating, rational characters are rewarded and the enthusiastic, impulsive ones are punished. But in neither is the educator prominent. On the contrary, Russell, a good educator who is a natural descendant of Frank's mother, plays a significant role in "Vivian," the logical step between "Madame de Fleury" and Miss Edgeworth's next large undertaking, *Patronage*. Vivian is a young man whose education has utterly failed; however, the responsibility for this failure is not the tutor's, the rational utilitarian Russell: "But I have had [Russell tells Vivian] the honour to be your guide, philosopher, and friend, only for these three years. . . . I believe in the rational, but not the magical power of education. How could I do, or undo, in three years, the work of the preceding seventeen?" Rather, the flaws in Vivian's education originate with his mother who "over-educated, over-instructed, over-dosed [him] with premature lessons of prudence" to the extent that he "had not eyes, ears, or understanding" of his own ("Vivian," p. 240). Thus he is the opposite of Virginia St. Pierre—he is over-educated. But he cannot act in a way that stronger, self-reliant people can trust, and, more importantly, Russell cannot teach him to be prudent. Like Basil, he is beyond the help of education.

Glistonbury Castle, the setting for most of the story, calls to mind the Georgian mansion at Edgeworthstown, a laboratory where children were subjected to experiments in education. But, unlike Edgeworthstown, there is no agreement among the experimenters. The castle is torn by advocates for three utterly incompatible kinds of education. Lady Sarah is trained under the puritanical and old-fashioned ideas of her mother. Lady Julia is placed under the impulsive guidance of an actress with a questionable background. Lord Lidhurst is educated by Russell. The results are, for the most part, chaotic. Miss Edgeworth was primarily interested in these results; she clearly pointed out that the child is good until he is exposed to whichever educator he happens to have. She then clearly revealed her opinion of the theory by showing what happens when a child, who has been exposed to a corrupting education, confronts society.

75

Lady Sarah's governess is a Miss Strictland, a morbidly inhibited termagant who can see no farther than the gilt edge of a family Bible. She, of course, has outspoken scorn for Lady Julia's "progressive education": "In this house there were two parties, each in extremes, and each with their systems and practices carried to the utmost excess. The partisans of the old and the new school were here to be seen at daggers-drawing. Lady Glistonbury, abhorrent of what she termed modern philosophy, and classing under that name almost all science and literature, especially all attempts to cultivate the understandings of women, had, with the assistance of her double, Miss Strictland, brought up Lady Sarah in all the ignorance and all the rigidity of the most obsolete of the old school; she had made Lady Sarah precisely like herself; with virtue, stiff, dogmatical, and repulsive; with religion, gloomy and puritanical; with manners, cold and automatic" ("Vivian," p. 333). Miss Strictland, like Hannah More, was in full agreement with the "Gentleman" of *Letters for Literary Ladies*.

In spite of this morbidly repressive training, Lady Sarah has a depth of feeling that puritanism did not touch. For example, she warmly defends her sister when the old women unfairly harass her for wishing to be in a small play. Also, her reserve breaks down at the very moment she needs it most. She thinks that Vivian, whom Lady Julia had already refused, will not propose to her, and with all the flourishes of a third-rate melodramatic heroine, she takes to her bed. Vivian, fool that he is, falls for this "attack." After their marriage, he further discovers, much to his dismay, that her deeply repressed sympathy erupts in violent displays of intense emotion: "After the loss of her mother [who died from over-fatigue from the wedding visits], Lady Sarah Vivian's whole soul seemed to be engrossed by fondness for her husband. In public, and to all eyes but Vivian's, her ladyship seemed much the same person as formerly: but, in private, the affection she expressed for him was so great, that he frequently asked himself whether this could be the same woman, who, to the rest of the world, and in every part of her life, appeared so cold and inanimate" ("Vivian," p. 404).

Vivian's inability to stand on his own was caused by over-education, but Lady Sarah's outbursts of emotion stemmed from a particular kind of over-education—repression of feelings. Her natural vivacity had been so atrophied that she utterly lacked self-control. Actually, these two depraved people deserved each other; if the

novel had been written in the twentieth century, they would probably have been quite happy in their own little perverted world.
But Miss Edgeworth could never have seen eye to eye with Henry
Miller; Lady Sarah repels her husband by her continual seizures of
emotion. In Miss Edgeworth's spinster imagination, no man wants a
wife who is empty-headed.

When Vivian dies, Lady Sarah returns to the prison of her mor-
bidity. She can no longer sympathize with other people, so she iso-
lates herself from them. Miss Edgeworth brilliantly analyzed the
effects of repression and deftly showed the outcome of an education
that sets as its primary goal the repression of passion. It is a shame
that she was not listened to more closely by the generations that
followed her. The puritanical school of the Hannah Mores, she
dramatically illustrated, fails to curb over-powering emotional outbursts and, therefore, causes unnecessary pain. The effect of such
education is to make the pupil utterly incapable of living in a sane
society.

The second kind of education that Miss Edgeworth dissected is
what we today call "progressive." Lord Glistonbury, a passionate
old man repelled by his wife's frigidity, "saw his own genius in
Julia; and he resolved, as he said, to give her fair play, and to
make her one of the wonders of the age." He places her under the
care of "a Miss Bateman; or, as he called her, *The Rosamunda*."
The woman is a third-rate actress who had failed on the stage and
who had—to say the least—questionable morals. In short, she is
scarcely the type of woman a well-balanced lord would hire to
educate his daughter. Lady Glistonbury does not let this willful
flaunting of her principles pass without loud tirades. She "objected
to Miss Bateman, as being of the class of literary women; to her
real faults, her inordinate love of admiration, and romantic imprudence, Lady Glistonbury did not object, because she did not at
first know them; and when she did, she considered them but as
necessary consequence of the *cultivation and enlargement of Miss
Bateman's understanding*" ("Vivian," p. 334). But Miss Bateman
stayed.

The already vivacious Lady Julia scoffs at her mother's sermons
on duty. In fact, she invites disgrace, because she does not know
how not to; she is completely uninhibited and utterly naïve. She
imprudently trusts Vivian, the man everyone knows cannot keep a
secret, with her secret attachment to Russell. Wild notions, like

Mary Wollstonecraft's "rights of women," may justify an emotional attraction while denying the demands of duty, but imprudence, Miss Edgeworth believed, trusts where prudence remains silent. Lady Julia is finally disowned by her family, but even then she is blinded by her impulses. Russell, she tells Vivian after he asked to marry her, "persuaded, by his eloquence compelled me to return to this castle. He took from me all hope; he destroyed by one word all my illusions—he told me that he loves another. He has left me to despair, to disgrace; and yet I love, esteem, and admire him, above all human beings!" ("Vivian," p. 367). Sent into exile with Miss Strictland (whose presence is, perhaps, a greater punishment than banishment alone), she ends, like her sister, as a recluse. Uninhibited emotions as well as repressed ones prevent healthy participation in the fashionable world. It is too corrupt to endure a Lady Sarah and too corrupting to insure a Lady Julia's honor. "Progressive education" is, therefore, as wrong in its way as the puritanical in another.

The third kind of education at Glistonbury Castle is rational utilitarianism. Miss Edgeworth, interestingly, associates Lord Lidhurst more with Lady Julia than with Lady Sarah. They are, for example, companions in life, and she nurses him in death. Also Lord Lidhurst's personality is closer to Lady Julia's than to their sister's. He is not inhibited, but the "judicious" educational doctrines of Russell still influence his actions. Russell is, of course, the rationalist described in *Practical Education* and in *Essays on Professional Education*; therefore, the death of his wards is a definite statement on his value as an educator and on the theory for which he stands. In Vivian's case, the irreparable damage of early training could not be overcome; Russell has some excuse for the failure (although Madame de Rosier and Miss Locke had had no trouble overcoming similar challenges). But in Lord Lidhurst's case, Russell has material not yet corrupted and still able to absorb the doctrine. In fact, there is little added to plot by having the young lord die; Miss Edgeworth was doing nothing other than stating her reservations against the doctrine she had done so much to propagate.

Significantly, Russell is the only character who wins the woman he loves and who finds domestic happiness. Thus, whether he communicates his rationalism to his pupils or not, he has a good life. Neither Miss Strictland nor Miss Bateman found any happiness at all. In other words, Russell is trying to communicate a doctrine that he has found satisfying in his own experience. His failure is not an inherent part of his message. Miss Edgeworth did not tell how he arrived at his particular views, but she successfully showed that the message cannot be given to another. Regardless of the merits of the educator and of his message, certain students simply will not learn, and others will be unable to utilize the lessons. Yet the educator can still be happy and have the pleasure that others strive for.

Miss Edgeworth's value judgments concerning these kinds of education were carefully qualified. She, first of all, established the four kinds: Vivian's, Lady Sarah's, Lady Julia's, and Lord Lidhurst's. Then she compared and contrasted them. Vivian's early training made him too conscious of possible faults before he was mature enough to cope with them; he cannot understand the ambiguous morality of the fashionable world. He is the fool in the story. Obviously Miss Edgeworth condemned this education just as her father had in *Practical Education* (see I, 239), and she had little patience with its result. Lady Sarah's education, however, was worse. Miss Edgeworth described this character with sympathy, but she abhorred the governess who could be instrumental in forwarding such unnecessary misery. On the other hand, she could not condone Lady Julia's imprudence, but she appears to have sympathized more with the education that recognizes the claims of the emotions than the one that utterly damns them. Otherwise she would not have made Lady Julia and Lord Lidhurst such close companions. Finally, she showed that rational utilitarianism is ultimately futile, except for the educator himself. She valued the idea but believed that it was simply impractical. Apparently, then, she wanted to find a position somewhere between Lady Sarah and Lady Julia, a position that could produce a pupil who was mentally healthy and morally sound. In "Vivian" she restated her basic problem and was on the way to a reconciliation of passion and reason. Now she believed that the rational utilitarian could be happy with his philosophy, although she did not quite understand how. This understanding was a new plateau in her treatment of the problem, and with this notion as a foundation, she escaped the dilemmas of *Popular Tales* as she moved into the final years of her career.

In "Madame de Fleury" and "Vivian" the author advocated the harmonious union of reason and passion that she suggested in

79

Belinda, but in both stories she also stated the difficulties that accompany this union. Sister Frances peacefully dies after she reconciles her religion and her lessons, but as an educator she ignores the passions in order to preserve the status quo. Russell also has achieved what appears to be a reconciliation in private life but is unable to communicate to his pupils. Thus, even though Miss Edgeworth believed that this union is the most satisfying way to life, she did not know how it could be taught. The educators who attempt to reconcile the extremes in their own lives are ineffectual teachers. Apparently such a union can be found only through experience, but Miss Edgeworth did not yet commit herself to any definite answer.

CHAPTER SIX

Having restated her opinions in "Vivian," Miss Edgeworth concentrated on the question that her father had overlooked in *Essays on Professional Education*. There he allowed that the boy who was intended for the army could freely indulge his imagination, the exercise of which he felt was totally incompatible with prudence. But if a family has two sons—one intended for the army and the other, let us say, for the clergy—how can the boys follow completely different courses of education under the same parents? The would-be cleric needs prudence more than imagination; the would-be soldier needs imagination at the expense of prudence. Mr. Edgeworth gives no ground upon which the two boys can live under the same roof. In short, the incompatibility of the different educations presumes that a parent cannot educate sons for different professions lest the influence from one boy contaminate the other. Miss Edgeworth faced this question in her most ambitious novel, *Patronage* (1814), where the question is advanced in her own terms. She described two sisters, one basically rational and the other basically imaginative, who are both influenced by rational utilitarianism. In addition, her treatment of these sisters makes *Patronage* the penultimate step in her reconciliation of passion and reason, for by concentrating on siblings, she dramatically showed that the two personalities do in fact coexist.

A brief outline of the plot of this long complicated novel cannot help but be confusing; nevertheless, a rough sketch of the most important events is necessary since so few people have read it. One night a Dutch ship wrecks near the Percys' estate; lost in the turmoil are M. de Tourville's secret state papers that later fall into the hands of Commissioner Falconer. The Commissioner uses these papers to place himself and his family under the patronage of the Prime Minister, Lord Oldborough. Meanwhile, the Percys' home burns and their deed to the estate is lost. Thus while the Falconers rise in the world, the Percys lose their estate because they no longer have proof of ownership. The Commissioner forces one son into the clergy, marries another to a rather frivolous young lady because the boy was a threat to his patron, and shows off his daughters at fashionable parties. Meanwhile, the Percys take their loss with philosophic calm. Lord Oldborough discovers a plot from the papers and sponsors the Falconers' continued rise in the fashionable world until he finds that Cunningham Falconer is engaged in a plot against him. At the same time, the Falconer girls are introduced to eligible bachelors but get no proposals while Caroline Percy refuses three suitors. Finally, Lord Oldborough discovers Mrs. Falconer in a plot against him and, having proved his innocence, resolves never to see the Falconers again. After this, the novel moves rapidly to a close. The deed is found; Lord Oldborough and the Percys become friends; and everyone who has been independent and prudent lives happily ever after.

The action of *Patronage* is divided between the well-educated Percy family and their cousins, the poorly educated Falconers. The characters, the families as a whole, and the doctrines of opposing philosophies are contrasted one to another so that the device of contrast becomes far more complicated than in anything else she wrote. Miss Edgeworth brought this elaborate pattern of contrast and counter-contrast to bear on the action that spells out the surface moral. Should a man, she asked on this level, rise in the world through the influence of patrons, or should he rise from merit alone? Her solution is ambivalent; she saw the validity of both sides of the question and suggested that the true answer lies somewhere between a simple yes or no reply. Mr. Percy, for example, tells one of his sons: "I hold it to be just and right, that friends should give, and that young men should gratefully accept, all the means and opportunities of bringing professional acquirements and abilities into notice. Afterwards, the merits of the candidate, and his fitness for any given situation ought, and probably will, ultimately decide whether the assistance has been properly or improperly given" (*Patronage*, II, 165-66). The Percys consistently emerge in a favorable light when contrasted to the Falconers. Miss Edgeworth clearly valued merit while she looked with suspicion on patronage without merit.

The question of patronage boils down to an analysis of independence from and dependence on society. The Percys thus refuse to sell their liberty and, by remaining independent, are ultimately rewarded. Their struggle to be recognized for merit is difficult and filled with temptations from would-be Chesterfields. On the other hand, the Falconers, lacking merit, become dependent and eventually are disgraced by the intrigue of society. The Percys repossess their estates and have domestic happiness; the Falconers are degraded by public disgrace, separation, court-martial, and poverty. On a rather simple level, adversity comes to the Percys until they prove themselves superior to their society, but this adversity, like the Christians' "vale of tears," is merely a testing ground for prudence. The temporary prosperity of the Falconers is also a test, but they fail because imprudence blinds them to the most secure means to preserve their status. They are ensnared by the corruption of an evil society. Only the uncorrupted, who remain independent of society, can calculate the future and overcome evil.

Still, Miss Edgeworth placed the Falconers in more dramatic situations and more fully developed them as well-rounded characters than she did the Percys. Their escapades and peccadillos give the plot what tension and suspense it has, for the Percys are much too philosophical to sustain interest through the four long volumes. The writer had learned that a prudent character is harder to draw than an unreasonable one, and in *Patronage* she expressed this difficulty: "Produce . . . only dare to produce one of your reasonable wives, mothers, daughters, or sisters in the theatre, and you would see them hissed off the stage.—Good people are acknowledged to be the bane of the drama and novel—I never wish to see a reasonable woman on the stage, or an unreasonable woman off—I have the greatest sympathy and admiration for your true heroine in a book; but I grant you, that in real life, in a private room, the tragedy queen would be too much for me; and the novel heroine would be the most useless, troublesome, affected, haranguing, egotistical, insufferable being imaginable" (*Patronage*, I, 210).

Miss Edgeworth, for example, sketched the personalities of her minor characters in fast, satirical strokes: "The Lady Arlingtons . . . are glad to get Mrs. Falconer, and Mrs. Falconer is glad to have them, because they are related to my Lord Duke. . . . The style and tone of the Lady Anne is languishing—of Lady Frances, lively—both seem mere spoilt selfish ladies of quality: Lady Anne's selfishness is of the cold, chronic, inveterate nature.—Lady Frances's, of the hot acute, and tormenting species.—She 'loves every thing by fits, and nothing long.'—Every body is *an angel* and a *dear creature*, while they minister to her fancies—and no longer.—About these fancies she is restless and impatient to a degree which makes her sister look sick and scornful beyond description.—Lady Anne neither fancies, nor loves any thing, or any body.—She seems to have no object upon Earth, but to drink barley-water, and save herself from all manner of trouble or exertion, bodily or mental.— So much for the lady Arlingtons" (*Patronage*, II, 360-61). But when she drew more rational major characters, she had difficulty. In fact, the characters drawn with the weakest lines are usually the ones who have the most praiseworthy personalities (at least from her father's point of view). When a Percy is contrasted to a Falconer, the Percy is believable only because the more earthy Falconer is used for his background. The result is that the irrational characters everywhere command the reader's attention.

If we briefly compare the author's portraits of Godfrey Percy and Buckhurst Falconer, we can clearly see how she turns this difficulty to advantage. Godfrey is courageous, rational, altruistic, and temperate. He is a rational utilitarian. But when she described his choice of a profession, Miss Edgeworth couched her praise in negative terms. "Godfrey did not enter into the army from the puerile vanity of wearing a red coat and an epaulette; nor to save himself the trouble of pursuing his studies; nor because he thought the army a *good lounge*, or a happy escape from parental control; nor yet did he consider the military profession as a mercenary speculation, in which he was to calculate the chance of getting *into the shoes*, or over the head, of Lieutenant A— or Captain B—. He had higher objects; he had a noble ambition to distinguish himself. Not in mere technical phrases, or to grace a bumper toast, but in truth, and as a governing principle of action, he felt *zeal for the interests of the service*" (*Patronage*, I, 158-59).

On the other hand, Miss Edgeworth described Buckhurst's behavior in positive terms. Buckhurst is the only character who struggles to discover himself. He is the father of an illegitimate child, weak, intemperate, disloyal, and rash. In his mental struggle to choose a profession, he is fully rounded as a character. It is interesting that his father wants him to be a clergyman and (in agreement with the edicts of *Essays on Professional Education*) forces him to take orders despite his own feelings. Miss Edgeworth portrayed Buckhurst's capitulation to his father's wishes in a soliloquy: "All his friends and acquaintances now joining in one chorus, told Buckhurst in courtly terms, that he was a fool, and Buckhurst began to think they might be right.—'For here,' said he to himself, 'are my two precious brothers finely provided for, one an envoy, the other a Major *in esse* and Lieutenant-colonel *in posse*—and I, *in esse* and *in posse,* what?—Nothing—but a good fellow—one day with the four-in-hand club, the next in my chambers, studying the law, by which I shall never make a penny. . . . No, no, I'll not make a galley-slave of myself.—Besides, at my mother's, in all that set, and in the higher circles with Hauton and the Clays, and those people, whenever I appear in the character of a poor barrister, I am scouted,—should never have *got on* at all, but for my being a wit— a wit!—and have not I wit enough to make my fortune? as my father says—What hinders me?—My conscience only—And why should my conscience be so cursedly delicate, so unlike other men's consciences?'—

"In this humor, Buckhurst was easily persuaded by his father to take orders" (*Patronage,* I, 287-88).

The account of this unfortunate choice is dramatic and moving, quite unlike the rather colorless description of Godfrey's choice. In fact, the capitulation of noble intentions to base ends is so much more emphatic that it eclipses the rational behavior contrasted to it. If Godfrey existed without Buckhurst, the novel would be a flat, wooden manipulation of puppets calculated to teach certain preconceived notions of correct behavior. But with Buckhurst to give Godfrey a place in the social world of the novel, Miss Edgeworth achieved verisimilitude in which the prudent character is acceptable because he is seldom seen. What she did here is the opposite of what Scott did four years later in *The Heart of Midlothian.* Scott shifted emphasis from the imprudent character, Effie Deans, by concentrating on her sister's struggle to save her life. In other words, he made the rational character *act* while he narrated the misfortunes of the irrational one. But Scott, though a better novelist, did not have Miss Edgeworth's double purpose.

Thus whenever Miss Edgeworth draws a hero who is a rational utilitarian, he is undramatic. After all, how dramatic can a person be who is intellectual and prudent and always calm? But she always turned this difficulty into a support for her own ideas. For example, many of the scenes that are supposed to illustrate rational utilitarianism are stilted, but the ones that demonstrate her own opinions are lucid, employing full encounter of passion and intellect. It is only in the total scheme of *Patronage* that rationality dominates.

The love story centers around two characters, Caroline Percy (the same Caroline of *Letters for Literary Ladies*) and Count

Altenburg (based in part on M. Edelcrantz), who clearly represent rational utilitarianism. Caroline is so calculating that she lacks emotional credibility in the first half of the novel. She carefully considers the merits and faults of her suitors, weighing each in a Benthamite balance before she decides whether she will allow herself to "fall in love." Likewise, Count Albert calculates Caroline's personality. He tests her reactions to trumped-up events and weighs her merits against her faults before he allows himself to become emotionally attracted. This type of personality is hardly material for an interesting love affair, but Miss Edgeworth was more interested in her own opinions than in a simple love affair. She created this calculating personality to show that it cannot escape emotions. Caroline's calculation and rationalism crumble before her overpowering emotional attraction to the count. The rational admonishment of her parents (the good educators in the novel) warns that she should not love before the man has spoken, but Caroline is haunted by his memory. Domestic occupations lose their savor, and she pines for him. Only after she marries him, does rationality reassert its strength. She calmly decides to remain with her father in debtors' prison while her husband returns to Germany.[1]

If Caroline represents the rationalist at the beginning of the novel, Rosamund, her sister, represents the emotionalist. Throughout the novel Miss Edgeworth contrasted the two sisters. Like Caroline, Rosamund endures adversity and in times of crisis follows the advice of her calculating parents. Yet she is impulsive, flighty, imaginative—a typical teenager. While Caroline carefully analyzes her suitors' personalities, Rosamund considers what dresses can be worn by the bridal party. The sisters are clearly representative of the opposites that Miss Edgeworth sought to reconcile.

The notes in the Slade copy of the first edition of *Patronage* are especially pertinent: "Miss R Percy was cousin german to little Rosamund in early Lessons (the author of Rivuletta)," and "No R. Percy was Little Rosamund. Laura fell over a wooden bridge and was drowned one day."

---

1. This episode, important in the first edition of *Patronage*, was later altered so that Caroline goes immediately to Germany with her husband. The sudden return of rationality was so unconvincing that Miss Edgeworth's alteration greatly strengthens the character and still demonstrates the futility of the rational utilitarianism.

In reply to a question concerning this cryptic riddle, Mrs. Richard Butler, the descendant of the Edgeworths who is now Miss Edgeworth's literary executor, concluded, "Why the 'author of Rivuletta' comes into the question I don't know. She was the beautiful Honora who died at 17, & was always understood to stand for Caroline Percy, & Maria for Rosamund" (Slade, p. 150). Apparently Miss Edgeworth saw herself as she described Rosamund both in the children's books and in *Patronage*, as predominantly emotional and imaginative. She was not the well-trained, rational child that Honora was, probably because her education was neglected until after her fifteenth birthday and because she was not as adaptable to change as the younger sister. As early as her first book she had timidly suggested that emotion was as important as judgment. Now, about twenty years later and much less timid, she showed in Caroline the result of attempting to be purely intellectual and in Buckhurst the result of being excessively emotional. Neither extreme is adequate, but Rosamund's personal reconciliation of the extremes is. Rosamund alone can grasp situations; she is obedient to her parents but acts with a free exercise of her imagination. When she falls in love, for example, she becomes rational. In the same way, Miss Edgeworth was obedient and able to become the rationalist when occasion demanded. Rosamund alone in Miss Edgeworth's gallery of characters is fully able to reason and to feel. Still the reconciliation that she sought was not complete.

In *Ormond*, the last book Miss Edgeworth wrote before her father's death, she reached the reconciliation that she had sought during the most productive twenty years of her career. She concentrated on the ideal imaginative personality who is willing and able to become rational when occasion demands.

In the preface, Mr. Edgeworth defended, for the last time, his comments on his daughter's fiction: "I have been reprehended by some of the public critics for the *notices*, which I have annexed to my daughter's works.—As I do not know their reasons for this reprehension, I cannot submit even to their respectable authority.—I trust, however, the British public will sympathise with what a father feels for his daughter's literary success, particularly as this father and daughter have written works in partnership.

"The natural and happy confidence reposed in me by my daughter puts it in my power to assure the public, that she does not write negligently—I can assert, that twice as many pages were written for these volumes as are now printed" (*Ormond*, I, i-ii). While this apologia belittled the charge that has most often been brought against him, the "partnership" has undoubtedly influenced *Ormond*, even though Mr. Edgeworth's revisions are not noticeable.[2] Still, Miss Edgeworth was determined to synthesize her doubts and her father's dogma. She gave *Ormond* a tighter structure than *Patronage* and avoided the surface didacticism that later critics feel marred most of her works. In fact, Mr. Edgeworth pointed out that "the moral of this tale does not immediately appear, for the author has taken peculiar care, that it should not obtrude itself upon the reader" (*Ormond*, I, iii).

Dividing characters into three groups—the educators, the pupils, and the rebels—Miss Edgeworth traced Ormond's progress from an unconditional belief in Rousseau's emotionalism to a symbolic acceptance of, and reconciliation with, Mr. Edgeworth's rationalism. Ormond's lack of education opposes him to Marcus, the son of his guardian: "Sir Ulick's fondness, however, had not extended to any care of [Ormond's] education; quite the contrary, he had done all he could to spoil him by the most injudicious indulgence, and by neglect of all instruction or discipline. Marcus had been sent to school and college; but Harry Ormond, meantime, had been let to run wild at home. . . . Harry's extremely warm, generous, grateful temper, delighted Sir Ulick, but he gloried in the superior polish of his own son. Harry Ormond grew up with all the faults that were incident to his natural violence of passions and that might necessarily be expected from his neglected and deficient education" (*Ormond*, II, 21-22). Like Lame Jervas, Ormond is free from affectation. As the innately good man who has not been corrupted, he possesses naïve nobility. On the other hand, Marcus has been corrupted: "Marcus, though he appeared a mild, indolent youth, was violent where his prejudices were concerned,—instead of being governed by justice in his conduct towards his inferiors, he took strong dislikes, either upon false information, or without sufficient examination of the facts—cringing and flattery easily won his favour; and on the contrary, any contradiction, or spirit even of independence in an inferior, he resented" (*Ormond*, II, 66-67). Miss Edgeworth always valued nobility more than sophisticated cun-

2. According to Miss Edgeworth, her father contributed to certain scenes in the novel (such as the death of King Corny) and "corrected the whole by having it read to him many, many times" (Oliver, p. 308).

ning; thus the outcome of the two boys' lives is not surprising. Ormond becomes increasingly noble; Marcus grows so cunning that he causes Sir Ulick's bankruptcy.

There are two rational educators in *Ormond*, Lady Annaly and Dr. Cambray. Because Lady Annaly believes that knowledge alone leads to prudence, she is scorned by the corrupt fashionable world. But she is not afraid of hostility and succinctly sums up her position by denying the power of fate: ". . . fate is an unmeaning commonplace—worse than commonplace word—it is a word that leads us to imagine that we are *fated* or doomed to certain fortunes or misfortunes in life.—I have had a great deal of experience, and I think, from all I have observed, that far the greatest part of our happiness or misery in life depends upon ourselves" (*Ormond*, II, 75). Between Lady Annaly and Dr. Cambray, Ormond is influenced by reason.

But he ultimately learns from experience. Impulsive behavior and emotional friends interrupt his rational lessons. For example, when Lady Annaly gives him a collection of books, King Corny tempts him with hunting or drinking. Thus Ormond's passion is never subjugated to a rational calculation. Literature itself prevents the rational influences from changing him. *Tom Jones*, a novel that Miss Edgeworth regarded as dangerously immoral, inflames his imagination, but he is led by his naturally good instincts and escapes immorality. On the other hand, when Lady Annaly introduces him to *Sir Charles Grandison*, he is not at first attracted to Richardson's sentimental didacticism but finally overcomes Fielding's bad influence. "The character of Sir Charles Grandison, in spite of his ceremonious bowing," Miss Edgeworth commented, "touched the nobler feelings of our young hero's mind, inspired him with virtuous emulation, made him ambitious to be a gentleman in the best and highest sense of the word" (*Ormond*, II, 173-74). With the good influence of Lady Annaly, Dr. Cambray, and Richardson, Ormond's excess is curbed. He remains imaginative and learns prudence.

Other pupils in the novel are Miss Annaly and Dora O'Shane. Miss Annaly is a rational utilitarian. As successful a product of her education as Henry Campbell in "The Good Aunt," she is so rational that she approaches love with a logarithmic table. In contrast, Dora is excessively emotional; she marries on the spur of the moment when the illusion of Parisian life overcomes her judgment.

89

Miss Edgeworth fully asserted her reconciliation of passion and reason through the interplay of these four pupils. Miss Annaly refuses Marcus' proposal because the prudent can penetrate the mask of the imprudent, however sophisticated, demonstrating that the corrupt product of formal training is inferior to the rational utilitarian. Later Miss Annaly refuses the proposal of the fashionable Colonel Albemarle and so escapes the degradation rashly chosen by Dora. Thus Miss Edgeworth advocated the superiority of the rational system to excessive emotionalism. Finally Miss Annaly accepts the proposal of Harry Ormond. The marriage is consummated in the Black Islands, an "Earthly Paradise" where King Corny had invited guests to gargantuan drinking sprees and where the pleasures of the hunt overshadowed literature. Thus Miss Edgeworth symbolically resolved the debate between reason and passion. She suggested that the greatest earthly rewards will come to such a union. Yet she did not attempt to dogmatize about it. It is as personal as marriage and is found only after experience has shown that it is superior to either reason or passion alone.

In her reconciliation of passion and reason, Miss Edgeworth was a precursor of the mid-Victorian Compromise. On one hand, she fully invited Madame de Staël's biting criticism, "Vraiment Miss Edgeworth est digne de l'enthousiasme, mais elle se perd dans votre triste utilité." On the other, she earned Macaulay's praise that equated her, rather illogically, with no less a literary giant than Homer. She took the didactic novel and molded it into a new form. But she did more. She spoke to her age and found willing listeners. She might have lacked the philosophical keenness of a David Hume, but she saw the mind of her contemporaries with as clear an insight as the Romantics who are still read. She spoke to the rising middle class that discarded rationalism with one hand and emotionalism with the other. In her fiction she balanced philosophy against philosophy and idea against idea just as her generation as a whole had been forced to do by the eruption in France. She sought what the great Romantics overlooked—a point where the conservative absolute and the liberal relatives might coexist. Through her search, she was led first to the dilemmas of *Popular Tales* and then to the compromise of *Ormond*. Her writings are, in one sense, a portrait of an age. She moved into the blind alleys of Romanticism and finally into the reconciliation of opposites that we now call Victorianism.

BIBLIOGRAPHY

ABRAMS, M. H. *The Mirror and the Lamp: Romantic Theory and the Critical Tradition.* New York, 1953.

ALLEN, WALTER. *The English Novel, a Short Critical History.* London, 1954.

ALTICK, RICHARD D. *The English Common Reader: A Social History of the Mass Reading Public, 1800-1900.* Chicago, 1957.

ANONYMOUS. "Patronage. By Maria Edgeworth," *Edinburgh Review,* XXII (1814), 416-34.

————. "*Tales of Fashionable Life.* By Miss Edgeworth," *Quarterly Review,* II (1809), 146-54.

ARMYTAGE, W. H. G. "Little Women," *Queen's Quarterly,* LVI (1929), 248-57.

BABBITT, IRVING. *Rousseau and Romanticism.* Boston, 1919.

BAKER, E. A. *The History of the English Novel.* Vol. VI. London, 1935.

BARBAULD, ANNA LETITIA. *Lessons for Children. In Four Parts.* Philadelphia, 1818.

BATE, W. J. *From Classic to Romantic.* New York, 1961.

BOOTH, WAYNE C. *The Rhetoric of Fiction.* Chicago, 1961.

BOSWELL, JAMES. *The Life of Samuel Johnson, L.L.D.* Modern Library Edition. New York, n.d.

BOYD, WILLIAM. *The Educational Theory of Jean Jacques Rousseau.* New York, 1963.

BRINTON, C. C. *English Political Thought in the Nineteenth Century.* Cambridge, 1949.

BUTLER, HARRIET JESSIE, and HAROLD EDGEWORTH (eds.). *The Black Book of Edgeworthstown and Other Memories, 1585-1817.* London, 1927.

————. "Sir Walter Scott and Maria Edgeworth. Some Unpublished Letters," *MLR,* XXIII (1928), 273-98.

CASSIRER, ERNST. *Rousseau, Kant, Goethe.* Trans. by James Gutmann, P. O. Kristeller, and John H. Handall, Jr. Princeton, 1945.

CHARPENTIER, JOHN. *Rousseau, the Child of Nature.* New York, 1931.

[CROKER, J. W.] "*Tales of Fashionable Life.* By Miss Edgeworth. Vols. 4, 5, and 6," *Quarterly Review,* VII (1812), 329-42.

DAVIDSON, THOMAS. *Rousseau and Education According to Nature.* "The Great Educators' Series." New York, 1898.

DAY, THOMAS. *The Dying Negro, a Poem,* 3rd ed. London, 1775.

————. *The History of Sandford and Merton.* Philadelphia, 1856.

DERATHÉ, ROBERT. *Le Rationalisme de J.-J. Rousseau.* Paris, 1948.

FAIRCHILD, H. N. *The Noble Savage: A Study in Romantic Naturalism.* New York, 1928.

FLANAGAN, THOMAS J. *The Irish Novelists, 1800-1850.* New York, 1958.

FLEISHER, DAVID. *William Godwin, a Study in Liberalism.* London, 1951.

FRANCIS, S. M. "Maria Edgeworth," *Atlantic Monthly,* XCVI (1905), 423-24.

GODWIN, WILLIAM. *Enquiry Concerning Political Justice and Its Influence on Morals and Happiness.* Ed. by F. E. L. Priestley. 3 vols. Toronto, 1946. [Photographic facsimile of the Third Edition corrected.]

GREY ROWLAND. "Heavy Fathers," *Fortnightly Review,* n.s., LXXXVI (1909), 80-89.

————. "Maria Edgeworth and Etienne Dumont," *Dublin Review,* CXLV (1909), 239-65.

————. "Society According to Maria Edgeworth," *Fortnightly Review,* n.s., LXXXII (1907), 296-308.

91

[HAYWARD, A.] "A Memoir of Maria Edgeworth, with a Selection from her Letters. By the late Mrs. Edgeworth," Edinburgh Review, CXXVI (1867), 458-98.

HUME, DAVID. A Treatise of Human Nature. Ed. by L. A. Selby-Bigge. Oxford, 1888.

JONES, O. McK. Empiricism and Intuitionism in Reid's Common-Sense Philosophy. Princeton, 1927.

KING-HELE, DESMOND. Erasmus Darwin. New York, 1963.

LAWLESS, EMILY. Maria Edgeworth. "The English Men of Letters Series." London, 1904.

LE BRETON, A. L. A Memoir of Mrs. Barbauld. London, 1874.

LOCKE, JOHN. An Essay Concerning Human Understanding. Ed. by A. C. Fraser. 2 vols. Oxford, 1894.

————. Some Thoughts Concerning Education. Ed. by Peter Gay. New York, 1964.

LOGAN, J. V. The Poetry and Aesthetics of Erasmus Darwin. Princeton, 1936.

LOVEJOY, A. O. The Great Chain of Being. New York, 1960.

METZ, RUDOLF. A Hundred Years of British Philosophy. Trans. by J. W. Harvey, T. E. Jessop, and Henry Sturt. New York, 1938.

MUNRO, DAVID H. Godwin's Moral Philosophy. London, 1953.

OSBORN, ANNIE MARION. Rousseau and Burke, a Study of the Idea of Liberty in Eighteenth-Century Political Thought. London, 1940.

PATERSON, ALICE. The Edgeworths, a Study of Later Eighteenth-Century Education. London, 1914.

POLLIN, B. R. Education and Enlightenment in the Works of William Godwin. New York, 1962.

PRAZ, MARIO. The Romantic Agony, 2nd ed. Trans. by Angus Davidson. London, 1951.

RAILO, EINO. The Haunted Castle, a Study of the Elements of English Romanticism. London, 1927.

RODDIER, HENRI. J.-J. Rousseau en Angleterre au XVIIIᵉ siècle, l'œuvre et l'homme. Paris, 1949.

RODWAY, A. E. Godwin and the Age of Transition. New York, 1952.

ROMILLY, SAMUEL H. (ed.). Romilly-Edgeworth, Letters, 1813-1818. London, 1936.

————. "The Lost Letters of Maria Edgeworth," Quarterly Review, CCLXVIII (1937), 103-17.

ROUSSEAU, JEAN-JACQUES. The Confessions. Trans. by J. M. Cohen. Baltimore, 1960.

————. Emile, ou de l'éducation. Œuvres de J.-J. Rousseau avec des notes historiques. Tomes VIII et IX. Paris, 1820.

————. Émile. Trans. by Barbara Foxley. London, 1911.

————. The First and Second Discourses. Trans. by Roger D. and Judith R. Masters. New York, 1964.

SADLER, M. E. Thomas Day, an English Disciple of Rousseau. Cambridge, 1928.

SAINT-PIERRE, BERNARDIN DE. Paul et Virginie. Paris, 1787.

SEWARD, ANNA. Memoirs of the Life of Dr. Darwin, Chiefly During his Residence in Lichfield, with Anecdotes of His Friends, and Criticisms on his Writings. Philadelphia, 1804.

STEPHEN, LESLIE. The English Utilitarians. 3 vols. London, 1900.

————. History of English Thought in the Eighteenth Century. 2 vols. New York, 1962.

STEVENSON, LIONEL. The English Novel, a Panorama. Boston, 1960.

STEWART, DUGALD. *Elements of the Philosophy of the Human Mind. The Collected Works of Dugald Stewart.* Vols. II and III. Ed. by Sir William Hamilton. Edinburgh, 1854.

TEXTE, JOSEPH. *Jean-Jacques Rousseau and the Cosmopolitan Spirit in Literature, a Study of the Literary Relations Between France and England During the Eighteenth Century.* Trans. by J. W. Matthews. London, 1899.

TREVELYAN, G. M. *British History in the Ninteenth Century, 1782-1901.* London, 1922.

WARD, WILFRED. "Moral Fiction a Hundred Years Ago," *Dublin Review,* CXLIV (1909), 245-66.

WARNER, J. H. "The Basis of Rousseau's Contemporaneous Reputation in England," *MLN,* LV (1940), 270-80.

———. "Émile in Eighteenth Century England," *PMLA,* LIX (1944), 773-91.

UNIVERSITY OF FLORIDA MONOGRAPHS

Humanities

No. 1: *Uncollected Letters of James Gates Percival,* edited by Harry R. Warfel

No. 2: *Leigh Hunt's Autobiography: The Earliest Sketches,* edited by Stephen F. Fogle.

No. 3: *Pause Patterns in Elizabethan and Jacobean Drama,* by Ants Oras

No. 4: *Rhetoric and American Poetry of the Early National Period,* by Gordon E. Bigelow

No. 5: *The Background of The Princess Casamassima,* by W. H. Tilley

No. 6: *Indian Sculpture in the John and Mable Ringling Museum of Art,* by Roy C. Craven, Jr.

No. 7: *The Cestus. A Mask,* edited by Thomas B. Stroup

No. 8: *Tamburlaine, Part I, and Its Audience,* by Frank B. Fieler

No. 9: *The case of John Darrell: Minister and Exorcist,* by Corinne Holt Rickert

No. 10: *Reflections of the Civil War in Southern Humor,* by Wade H. Hall

No. 11: *Charles Dodgson, Semeiotician,* by Daniel F. Kirk

No. 12: *Three Middle English Religious Poems,* edited by R. H. Bowers

No. 13: *The Existentialism of Miguel de Unamuno,* by José Huertas-Jourda

No. 14: *Four Spiritual Crises in Mid-Century American Fiction,* by Robert Detweiler

No. 15: *Style and Society in German Literary Expressionism,* by Egbert Krispyn

No. 16: *The Reach of Art: A Study in the Prosody of Pope,* by Jacob H. Adler

No. 17: *Malraux, Sartre, and Aragon as Political Novelists,* by Catharine Savage

No. 18: *Las Guerras Carlistas y el Reinado Isabelino en la Obra de Ramón del Valle-Inclán,* por María Dolores Lado

No. 19: *Diderot's Vie de Sénèque: A Swan Song Revised,* by Douglas A. Bonneville

No. 20: *Blank Verse and Chronology in Milton,* by Ants Oras

No. 21: *Milton's Elisions,* by Robert O. Evans

No. 22: *Prayer in Sixteenth-Century England,* by Faye L. Kelly

No. 23: *The Strangers: The Tragic World of Tristan L'Hermite,* by Claude K. Abraham

No. 24: *Dramatic Uses of Biblical Allusion in Marlowe and Shakespeare,* by James H. Sims

No. 25: *Doubt and Dogma in Maria Edgeworth,* by Mark D. Hawthorne

DATE DUE